Dressing Up

MARISA

Dressing Up

How to Look and Feel Absolutely Perfect for Any Social Occasion

Foreword by
DIANA VREELAND

Photographs by
BERRY BERENSON

ILLUSTRATIONS BY
MICHAEL COOPER

STYLISTS
ROSS BURMAN
KAREN MATTHEWS

G. P. PUTNAM'S SONS, NEW YORK

BERENSON

DESIGNED BY HELEN BARROW

LIBRARY OF CONGRESS CATALOGING IN PUBLICATION DATA

Berenson, Marisa, date.
Dressing up.

1. Clothing and dress.   I. Title.
TT507.B437 1984   646'.34   84–9769
ISBN 0–399–13003–9

ACKNOWLEDGMENTS

FIRST, my appreciation to my agent, Alfred P. Lowman of Authors and Artists Group, who persevered with his love and energy at all times.

A special thanks to my editor, Diane Reverand, who went beyond the call of duty and was so wonderful to work with.

My deep gratitude to Edith Loew Meyers, who helped me in the beginning.

And a very special thanks to my dear friend Connie Church, who was there for me and helped me pull it all together in the end.

Thanks to my husband, Richard, and my daughter, Starlite, both of whom support and inspire me in everything I do.

Thanks to hairstylists Oribe, NYC, and Rocky, NYC, and makeup artists Rudi Muñoz and Arnold Pipkin for their expertise and help during the shooting of this book.

And I'd like to thank the following people for their contributions:

Evening wear/Sportswear: Halston, NYC; Oscar de la Renta, NYC; Valentino, NYC; Saint Laurent-Rive Gauche, NYC; Roberto Fabris, courtesy of Lina Lee, NYC; Bob Mackie, courtesy of Lina Lee, NYC; Stephen Sprouse, NYC; Anthony Wong, NYC.

Lingerie: WifeMistress, NYC; Fernando Sanchez, NYC.

Shoes: Susan Bennis/Warren Edwards, NYC; Maud Frizon, NYC; Mario Valentino, NYC; La Marca, NYC; Manolo Blahnik, NYC; Valentino, NYC.

Jewelry: Wendy Gell, NYC; Richard Serbin, NYC; Tess Designs, NYC; Marla Buck, NYC; Good As Gold, NYC; Valentino, NYC.

Belts: Tess Designs, NYC; Barry Kieselstein-Cord, NYC.

Handbags: Morris Moskowitz, NYC.

Masques: Brett Lewis, NYC.

Properties: Fiberglass props—Niedermaier, Inc., NYC; art deco furniture—The Second Coming Ltd., NYC; art deco objets d'art—As Time Goes By, NYC; art nouveau hand mirror and brush set—Primamore, NYC.

Flowers: Florabund.

❧

For my grandmother,
"Schiap" (Elsa Schiaparelli),
who passed on to me
her wonderful sense of style.

8

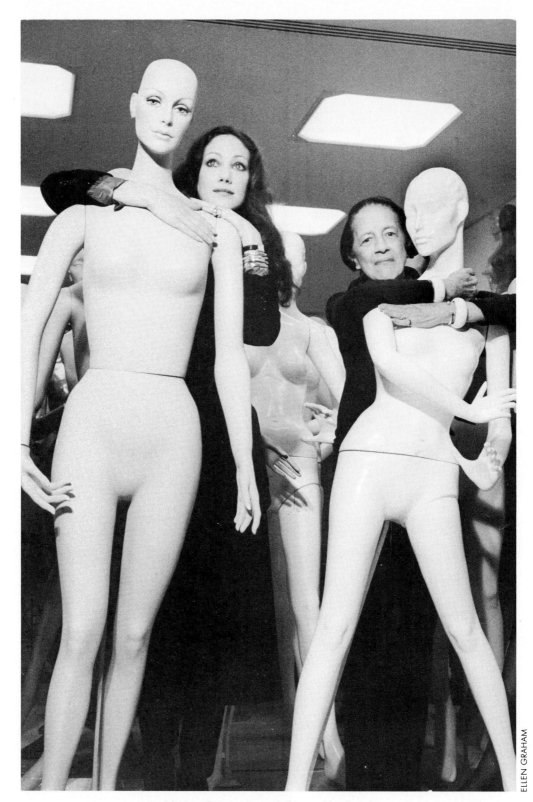

Marisa Berenson and Diana Vreeland

ELLEN GRAHAM

FOREWORD

I'VE KNOWN Marisa Berenson since she was a little girl. She grew up in the delicious snowy country of the Swiss Alps—all too beautiful for words. Very pure. And a wonderful place for a child to dream; a child who was going to come into the great world and into her inheritance as the granddaughter of Elsa Schiaparelli, a great couturiere and an adventuress in color. Marisa gets her great elegance and love of color from her grandmother. And she is one of the finest models I have ever worked with at *Vogue*. It's natural that Marisa, with her attraction to the beautiful things in life, wants to share her point of view on dressing up. It's *time*, as we are all a little bit tired of dressing down.

I think dressing up is a physical act—*absolutely*. First of all, you've got to clean up. You've got to take a big bath. You've got to be excited because you're having a *bath*. You've got to be excited because you're drying yourself. You've got to be excited before you put on your scent.

Then you've got to be excited about what you're going to wear. And it takes a bit of time, all this planning . . . thinking of the earrings, the special *parure*, which translates to "your accessories"—the bracelets or whatever you're going to wear with everything else. You've got to put a lot of physical stuff into it—energy and lust and *enthusiasm!*

I do think that dressing up is a physical *shot* for you. You feel better. You know you *look* better. Physically, you are *better*. It doesn't involve vanity at all; it's entirely about *exuberance*. And it's almost an athletic feat—your throat gets smaller and your neck gets longer and your hair gets better.

I can't imagine dressing up for anything except pleasure. It's one of the great pleasure-giving things, and I like to please people. But do many people want to please people? I think they want admiration, but do they want to *please* people? I know that I do. I want to please men. I want to please the people I work with.

This is all so natural to a Frenchwoman—to dress to please, to take care of herself, basically, in a way that has to do with being a woman. The American doesn't feel female enough; she's not on the *prowl*. She's too busy competing, which, of course, is the most devastating thing when it comes to dressing. Then you lose any individuality that God might have given you at birth. You're only competing with an advertisement you've seen in a magazine or something you've seen in the street.

Unfortunately, people start to be copyists at about twelve, and they lose their imagination. They lose the *dream* of *themselves*, and they start to try to get popular instead. Now, popularity is the middle lane, and not even the top middle lane: it's the barrier just above the slow lane. To be in the fast lane, you've got to keep what you've got, you've got to hold on to the dream. In other words, you have got to have a *great sense of yourself!*

As for the doubt about what to wear, that's a detail. Your dress is a detail. But your *eyes*. . . ! And your *parure*—that is not a detail, that *is* the point.

Of course if you're a shopper you're not dressed properly. Too much is available, you see too much, you get jammed up in your mind. Whereas dressing up is a thing that *comes* to you—you feel something and you go along with it. There's no pressure on you, you're not competing. You're dressed entirely the way you want.

I think that people can very easily become clothes-conscious, if they keep everything down to the *minimum*. Don't get too many *ideas*. Don't depend on too many *clothes*. Start with the basics, and work on your looks and your personality and your *walk*. We all admire a perfect body, but I much more admire a perfect walk. That's style, you see: a great walk and great carriage.

Then the dress. You might change the dress—you know, "I'm just going to pull on a white tunic over these black pants, that would be *much* better—with the rubies!" Then everything sort of takes its place. And you find yourself, say, putting your glasses in your belt—I mean, that's twenty years old, but that's the sort of spontaneity that goes with the exuberance of the hour, of the privilege, of the fun.

And then there's the whole picturesque side . . . You wrap your head like a nun. You wrap your head like a Turk. You don't wrap your head, you let everything *fl-y-y-y!* Or tear everything away and just wear earrings, or a tiara. I mean, the variety in it! It's contagious within oneself, what one wants to do. And there's no end—there's no stopping it once it goes!

Now, I said that people have too many clothes, and I'm sticking with that. Change your *stockings*—wear other-colored stockings and change your whole look! To me, the most démodé thing is this: I say to a woman, "God, that's a smart dress." "Oh, my dear," says she, "it's last year's," and I am supposed to faint. It's maddening!

I think you should be able to go two or three years without buying *anything.* But maybe you need a new *haircut.* Maybe you ought to pay a hundred dollars for a terribly good cosmetician to teach you how to make up.

Obviously, I'm talking basics—to *start.* As for the *extras,* you must splurge every now and then—"By gum, I'm going to buy that cerise-colored dress with the cherries on it!"—and you'll find it's the most practical thing you own. And of course, you put things away that you can bring out later. The other day I saw a little quilted bed jacket. I thought, God, if I were smart I'd pick that up! It was flowered cotton, and, I mean, it was suitable for the *bed.* Well, you put a little dead mink on it and you've got an awfully cute jacket to wear around the house of an evening.

When Hollywood dressed up, people *adored* it. It was the glamour capital of the world—the *world,* don't forget—not just America. Garbo is part of history. Dietrich is part of history.

You know, I'm part of that extraordinary time—the great time. All my friends were extraordinary. All the clothes were so beautiful. It was the time . . . it was like a cup holding all of us.

12   We've had a little too much dressing down, don't you think? And for whom are you dressing down? You bore men, you bore the people in the street. I say *give 'em something!* Give 'em something they never knew they'd ever get. Give them all the splash and the champagne, all the caviar.

If you want to play it safe, go ahead and play it safe. There are dozens of very good fashion books that will tell you how to do it. But this isn't one of them. Marisa has a great sense of stacking it on, pouring it on, wrapping herself up and getting the right temperature at the right time all of the time. It is her gift to be able to make things picturesque and perfect for the moment.

In this book, Marisa shares a champ's view of dressing up and being a bit gala, and that's what I'm for, too. We *need* the gala. We need the joie de vivre; without joie de vivre you have nothing. You can't want to please someone unless you have a sense of joy. You can't *really* want *anything* unless you have a sense of joy . . . and a sense of fun . . . and a sense of love.

DIANA VREELAND

CONTENTS

Here and on the next eight pages, furs for every hour—mink paled for day...
the little black ermine dress...black asymmetries...marvellous new brown
furs. Here, two delicious furs for evening, and extravagant, dazzling heads.
Left: Short chinchilla cape wrapped high...slit to show an arm in black
suède pavé with brilliants. Feathering the head, a sunburst of burnt
peacock feathers, one huge rhinestone globe glittering in the centre.
Cape of Empress chinchilla, made to order by Maximilian. Hat by
Halston, made to order at Bergdorf Goodman. The gloves by
Kislav. Earrings by Joseph Warner. Both at Best & Co.
Right: Giant triangle of white ermine curving over the
shoulders...pointed straight to the back of the knees.
Coquetry supreme: bogus pearl ropes swinging from the
head like a harem curtain of heads. Wrap of white
Canadian ermine by Petrovits & Tepper. Necklace
by Valjean: Tailored Woman. Schreiner ring.

OF THE NIGHT: SOFT LITTLE SHRUGS... DAZZLING HEADS

Vogue *modeling days, 1965.*

NEWTON / VOGUE

INTRODUCTION

I THINK it's fabulous to be a woman because no matter how much we achieve, regardless of how many ladders we climb, we are still women and we get to celebrate our femininity by dressing up.

I love dressing up and all of the elegance and allure that is a part of it. Think of the visions that you can create and the fun you can have doing it. A woman is so lucky to have a chance at fantasy and a chance to *play* for real.

Women love the idea of their own femininity. I can't think of anything that makes a woman feel prettier or more complete than lavishing on the jewels, the silk, the perfume; of going for all of it and dressing up for all it's worth. And for most women, the little extra effort it takes is as natural as breathing.

So why does the thought of dressing up for a night on the town cause such anxiety, as though it were an adventure into the unknown? Well, dressing up—really doing a number—*is* an adventure, but not all that unknown. It's not all that different, in fact, from the way we played as children, dressing up in our mothers' clothes, piling on jewels and scarves, indulging whims and fancies, experimenting with outrageous makeup—inventing ourselves, so to speak, out of our own imagination.

We saw a lot of that spirit come into fashion in the sixties—and blow out again in the seventies. Now, I think, we're beginning to realize what a lot of fun and glamour we've been missing—discreetly tailored (by which I absolutely do not mean man-tailored) is a great way to be by day, but there *is* life after business.

And I believe that inside many, many grown-up women that childlike spirit of dressing up is just screaming to get out—to amuse, to delight, to beguile, to give pleasure to themselves and to others. To knock 'em dead, in a word—but never to shock. To be outrageous is one thing (for most evenings a terrific thing, I think); to outrage is something else again.

Dressing up means rising to both the mood and the etiquette of the evening, so that the way you look causes a little stir without raising a single eyebrow: "Goodness, doesn't she look pulled together and fabulous!"

And that brings us to something called personal style, which can't be bought from even the most gifted designer. Of course it's wonderful to be dressed by a Saint Laurent or a Halston or a Valentino; the very name on the label is an imprimatur of correctness. But personal style goes beyond fashion; it has to do entirely with you and the way you project—with clothes and makeup and accessories and jewels—not a magazine ideal of the latest fashion, but your own image of who you are and how you want to be seen.

Dressing with personal style has also to do with being absolutely unintimidated by fashion. If you own a daytime black pants suit, for instance, even if it's a Saint Laurent pants suit, you don't hesitate to pull it apart and put the jacket over a slinky, slit skirt for evening, or wear the pants with a knockout jeweled sweater, or wear the pants and jacket with nothing underneath but a million marvelous necklaces. Or, if all the clothes in your closet suddenly vanished, and you were left with only jeans, a sweatshirt, a pair of sexy shoes, and a ton of costume jewelry, you would not for one second dream of calling your hostess and saying you can't possibly come to cocktails. You'd put yourself together with what you've got and go to town! I certainly would.

I've been dressing up all of my life. Obviously, being a model (which I was) or an actress (which I am) is perfect training for this sort of thing—you have to be inventive with what you've got or you'd go broke shopping. Neither, of course, did it hurt to have a great couturiere for a grandmother, because it meant having the most exquisite christening dress imaginable (in which I made my first appearance in *Vogue*).

Vogue *modeling days, 1967. "Even then I loved dressing up with lots of jewels."*

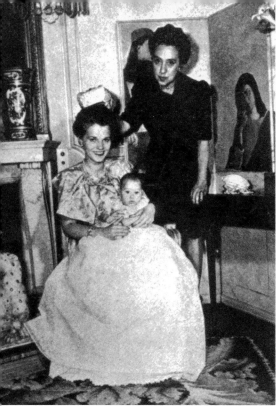

Here I am making my first appearance in Vogue—wearing my christening gown—with my mother and grandmother.

Elsa Schiaparelli

HORST / VOGUE

Dressing Up *with my sister Berry in shocking-
pink wool coats and bonnets designed by
grandmother Schiaparelli. That's Mother keeping
an eye on us.*

*Berry and I dressed up in Christmas
party dresses that "Schiap"
designed for us.*

L. KAZAN / CHEVALIER

Marisa and Berry: two different women each with her own sense of style.

But apart from such grandmotherly benevolence, Elsa Schiaparelli was a fantastically innovative designer who gave the world embroidered sweaters and jackets, shocking pink and shoulders out to there. More than anything, she brought to her work wit and audacity—and great fantasy—that knocked the stuffiness right out of fashion.

It was in the rebellious spirit of my grandmother that I left home at sixteen. I came to the United States under the wing of fashion doyenne Diana Vreeland and became a top *Vogue* model. From modeling, I pursued an acting career. I landed starring roles in *Death in Venice, Cabaret, Barry Lyndon, SOB, Playing for Time,* and most recently, *The Secret Life of Sigmund Freud* and *Desire.*

When I was asked to host the fashion industry's prestigious Coty Awards for 1983, my first thought was what fabulous outfit would my grandmother want me to wear! Obviously something fantastic and fun, which is how I've always felt dressing up should be for everyone.

There are lots of things in this world that one has to be serious about. I don't think dressing up is one of them. Dressing up is about fun and flirt and glamour—and being a little creative with yourself.

MARISA BERENSON

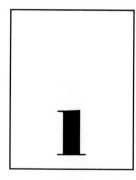

DRESSING TO THE OCCASIONS

LET'S START with a simplifying fact: wherever in the world you happen to be—excepting, maybe, on safari in Africa or a sleigh tour around the Arctic tundra—there are basically only four degrees of evening for which you will ever be dressing up. In order of descending formality, they are as follows:

The white-tie evening, so called for the white tie and tails that were once (and in some cases still are) de rigueur for men at diplomatic receptions, occasions of state and the grandest of weddings. Put on your best ball gown—this is the most elegant of occasions.

The black-tie evening, named, as above, for what the men are expected to wear—in this case black tie and dinner jacket (also known as a tuxedo). "Black tie" on an invitation—or even "black tie (or dress) optional"—indicates that what the host has in mind is not quite as formal as white tie, but very, very dressy just the same. A lovely long dress is appropriate. This includes opening night at the opera, season opening of the symphony, all the balls—debutante, inaugural. In other words, your average stops-out, star-studded, super-big gala: an *event.* Into this category also fall largish but private dinner parties, with or without dancing, theater openings, film premieres, some art exhibits (e.g., a museum preview scheduled for around

7 P.M.), benefit performances, fund-raising dinners, evening wedding receptions, evenings where you start with a cocktail party at a private house and go on to a more elaborate party elsewhere. An extravagant short dress is appropriate.

Dress optional means you choose. I would go for the dressier look. A safe range would be anything from a pair of evening pants and silk shirt or embroidered sweater to a short, dressy evening dress. Nothing daytime. If you

opt out, you will probably hate yourself in the morning because every other woman there is sure to be dressed to the teeth.

The "little evening"—a catchall phrase for the wide-ranging category of evening that you find yourself dressing for most of the time: cocktail parties, open-house parties, dinner at a restaurant, the theater, the ballet, a concert, nightclubs, discos—really an evening where no dress code is specified but you do want to look rather nice, even a little bit sensational.

Now. Having established a hierarchy of occasions, let's take a look at the reality. The truth of the matter is that a certain flexibility has carried over from the sixties—a kind of *laisser-aller* attitude that has survived to the eighties. You can therefore expect to see men in black tie at white-tie evenings, in dark business suits at black-tie evenings, or, conversely (because men also like to dress up once in a while), in black tie and dinner jacket at restaurants, at relatively informal parties, or at any of the little evenings mentioned above.

And at every one of these evenings—short of the very biggest, when you

New York Mayor Ed Koch's Ball, 1981. This elegant velvet suit is a great look for "dress optional." Always appropriate.

This is a great black-tie look when dressing for a younger crowd or a night out in Hollywood.

really have got to pull out *all* the stops—you will see women in short dresses as well as long, pants as well as dresses, the simple as well as the spectacular.

Although my preference is for short dressy dresses, there are times when I would never wear a short dress. They are: any big ball, the season opening at the opera, and big political functions (especially in Washington).

Tip: Remember that the long dress is popular with the older crowd, while the short dress tends to be more youthful.

In 1983, when I hosted the Coty Awards, the fashion industry's Oscars, an event that is literally the height of fashion, I saw every degree of dressing,

This was a great little "night on the town" look. The hat gave the perfect touch.

DUSTIN PITTMAN / WOMEN'S WEAR DAILY

from all-out to what would have been more appropriate to a day at the office. However unintentional, there is a point at which dressing down is rude, as though the occasion were not worth the effort.

My own feeling is, if you want to do a big number for a little evening, do it. The chances of being overdressed are slim, and underdressing isn't going to give you (or anybody who sees you) nearly the lift.

KNOW THE TERRITORY

I have never, ever felt overdressed, but I can remember an occasion when I definitely felt underdressed. It was my first time at the White House—a dinner for Giscard d'Estaing, during the Ford administration. What I wore was a wispy little black chiffon handkerchief of a dress, short in front, long in back and wrapped like a sarong. I had little diamonds in my ears and a diamond bracelet. Not enough dress. Not enough jewelry.

Or, rather, not enough for this particular setting. I'd have been fine at a black-tie dinner at someone's house, or at one of the Vreeland fashion-show openings at the Metropolitan Museum, where almost anything goes as long as it's glamorous.

What I should have known—would have known if I had thought to check with someone who did—is that Washington is a fairly conservative town that loves to dress up in the most traditional sense of the word. Anything less than a long, "important" dress isn't quite going to do it for you. In Washington, Mies van der Rohe to the contrary, less is less.

Tip: Know the territory. If you don't, find out. Ring up your hostess or a friend who's going to be there—or has been there. It will save you time and worry in advance, regrets—and possibly embarrassment—afterward.

Speaking of which . . . Do you remember, in the sixties, when every other thing that came into fashion—the monokini, the topless bathing suit, the transparent top—was as much a dare as something to wear? I couldn't quite see myself topless, but being young, with a good figure, and not too much bosom, I adored the idea of the transparent, see-through top, especially Saint Laurent's.

One night, I wore what I thought was a fairly modest version to a very proper black-tie dinner at a rather grand house in Paris. The top was black lace, so not as revealing as just a couple of layers of chiffon, but, nevertheless, revealing.

Naturally, every man in the room, twenty to seventy, was gaga, and the few younger women present couldn't have been less perturbed. But it was largely an older crowd, and for every delighted older man, there was a conspicuously undelighted older woman, including the hostess, who, I'm sure, would have had me taken out and shot directly following the soup course, if it could have been managed discreetly.

THE RULES OF THE GAME

The point is, although dress codes today are relaxed in the extreme, there is still an observable etiquette. So . . . rule of thumb: *don't* dress in a way that might be seen as a challenge to other guests or a flouting of their conventions.

32

Do, if you know (and you will if you've done your homework) that it's going to be an older and/or conservative crowd, skip the ultra-bare, ultra-short—a little tact turneth away wrath.

Tip: Consider the following "appropriateness" questions before dressing up:

- What is the age of the crowd?
- What are their professional types?
- What event are we all dressing for?
- What will *I* feel most comfortable in?
- What is the image that I want to project?

OUTRAGEOUS WITHOUT CREATING OUTRAGE

There are going to be times when you do want to look outrageous, to get done up in a real attention-getter. You may be making your entrance on a stage or just down a staircase. You want some leg to show. You want to look really glamorous. So you dress to the nines and look fabulous.

When I did the Césars (the French Oscars) in Paris, I wore a breathtaking off-the-shoulder black velvet number with wonderful black feathers and a slit up to *here.* As if that weren't enough, I also wore a huge diamond necklace and earrings. Everybody said I was the best-dressed there.

A designer friend asked me to wear a gorgeous, transparent chiffon, showing every inch of the body underneath. But I felt that this would have been wrong for me. I am past the age where I feel comfortable in a dress like that—in fact it would have been an outrage for me to wear it. The black velvet dress that I wore was outrageous (outrageously gorgeous) without being shocking. I felt fabulous in it, I was noticed and I definitely made a statement.

WHEN BUSINESS IS PLEASURE

A word about the office party—the after-office-hours or out-of-the-office variety—at which the question of tact is *crucial.* Don't fool yourself. The distinctions that exist at the office still obtain. Be tactful and resist the drop-dead effect. It could make the junior assistant feel like a little gray wren, the boss's wife feel uneasy, and cause the client to wonder if this is quite the image he (she) wants to project.

Again, the better part of valor is to avoid the ultra. Otherwise, treat the office party as you would any glamorous little evening. If you don't have time to go home and change, plan on bringing a change of accessories: sexy little shoes, different jewels, maybe a little jacket. Do not—repeat, *not*—come as you were at 9 A.M.

As for the office party during office hours and on office premises, that's easy: don't wear anything you wouldn't wear on an ordinary office day (i.e., forego chiffon, sequins, glitz); do, however, give it an extra-pretty turn. Wear your everyday pullover, for instance, with a matching skirt or pants (the pulled-together way to wear separates)—black, say—with big earrings, bracelets, corals and pearls at the neck, and a black pin-striped jacket with souped-up shoulders.

CONVENTIONAL WISDOM

Then there's the business convention, which you, for sundry qualities in which your company takes pride, have been elected to attend. Keep in mind: when you are sent on such a mission, you aren't entirely a private person. In effect, you're the company's ambassador—their best foot forward. It doesn't mean that you have to make drastic changes in your own style—after all, they wouldn't be sending you if they didn't like it—but do respect theirs, as well: is it staid? permissive? somewhere in between?

It's like auditioning, actually. If I were up for the lead in *Jane Eyre,* I wouldn't go to the reading in a silver-fox chubby and character shoes!

WHEN BELLS ARE RINGING

Since evening is what we're about, let's skip the strictly morning wedding and move right along to the afternoon reception and the evening wedding.

The reception, although it may start earlier than the usual cocktail party, is, in effect, precisely that. The trick is to be as festive as possible—but just a shade less than if you were dressing for evening. This is the occasion when you would be grateful for a Chanel-type suit in your wardrobe, or, for that matter, any very pretty, very feminine suit that you can put a beautiful soft blouse with and masses of jewlery.

Or you can put it together with separate pieces. Recently, for example, I went to a friend's three o'clock wedding reception dressed this way: patch-work leather jacket—mostly in reds, turquoise, black and gold—a black skirt, turquoise silk shirt, turquoise satin shoes and turquoise gloves. (I love that punch of color.)

Evening weddings shouldn't cause a moment's concern, if you remember one thing: you have been asked to an evening party of the most gala kind! My own wedding was white tie all the way—men in tails, women in long dresses. My sister, Berry, wore red sequins, and I was in pink silk taffeta, strapless, fitted to the hip, then a gorgeous *whoosh* of skirt to the floor.

WHEN IT'S YOUR PARTY

Cocktail party, dinner party, open house—whatever: if it's happening at your place, dressing for it is the same as dressing for a party at anybody else's place.

To me, this means a short dressy dress or dressy pants. It almost never means a long dress. There is something about being at home in a long dress that just doesn't do it for me. Perhaps if I were living in a terribly grand house and giving a terribly grand dinner party, with *placements,* and so forth—but that isn't the way most of us live, and certainly not in this country. In the context of the way we do live, a long dress in one's own place seems a bit stuffy and pretentious, unless you're giving a little dinner first and going on to a ball.

Neither am I mad about caftans. I know a lot of women are (especially

California women), because they're so easy—you pop it on and you're dressed. But you lose your body, and you lose your legs. The real McCoy is another story: those ravishing silk robes from China and the bejeweled and embroidered caftans, with silken cords to wrap the waist, that one finds in such places as Marrakesh and treasures forever. They are to die over!—and to wear at home whenever you can.

HOLIDAY OCCASIONS

Having pretty well disposed of long dresses at home, I must tell you that I reverse myself completely when it comes to special holidays. Even if it's only a few close friends gathered together at one or the other's house to see in the New Year, I think everybody ought to dress up to beat the band—men in black tie and women in whatever makes them feel most glamorous: if a long dress is what does it for you, do it!

WHEN IN ROME

Rome, Paris, London—in any sophisticated European city, you can expect a more formal mood than in the States. A sit-down dinner for at least twenty people, mid-week, at a friend's flat in Paris may find the host in black tie, the hostess in a long dress, and the guests dressed in keeping. You could get away with a short dress, but I think you'd feel more sanguine about the evening in a long one. A silky black jersey, for example, folds up like a sigh in your suitcase, and it's going to look right anywhere.

Also to remember: whether you're traveling for business or pleasure, you're probably going to be going out more than you do at home—pack accordingly.

Tip: A few dressy separates—a short skirt, pants, a couple of nifty sweaters and blouses, and a marvelous jacket—will give you as many different looks as a whole bunch of dresses, in half the packing space. Also, one great short dressy dress is a must.

Tip: Don't fool around with the unfamiliar. *Do* take with you only the stuff you *know* you enjoy dressing up in. It's not much fun to find that you're stuck with a lemon and no time to do anything about it.

2

THE BASICS

WHEN IN DOUBT, GRAB BLACK

A DISCLAIMER FIRST. I adore color. I've always worn lots of it, often all at once—pale pink with shocking pink and red and purple. That's something my grandmother did. Schiap was famously—outrageously—daring with color: five different reds at a time, with maybe a shot of green. And you'd have killed to own it, the look was so sensational.

Schiap was just as famous, however, for black. Basic black. As in *little black suit.* As in *little black dress.* The most important thing for a woman to have in her wardrobe, she said, and so do I.

That little black dress, for instance. Let's say you owned one—day length, bone simple. Maybe it's wool jersey, or silk jersey, or cotton jersey, like a T-shirt. Or maybe it's a cashmere sweater extended to dress length. Maybe it's crepe de chine and cut all on the bias.

Anyway, you own this little black dress. And you wear it belted, you wear it unbelted, you wear it six ways from Sunday: as a tunic over pants; as a short blouson, pulled way up and held low around the hips with a big soft sash, which gives you the look of a flounce; or you just wear it belted, with lovely jewels and textured hose, for a classic look.

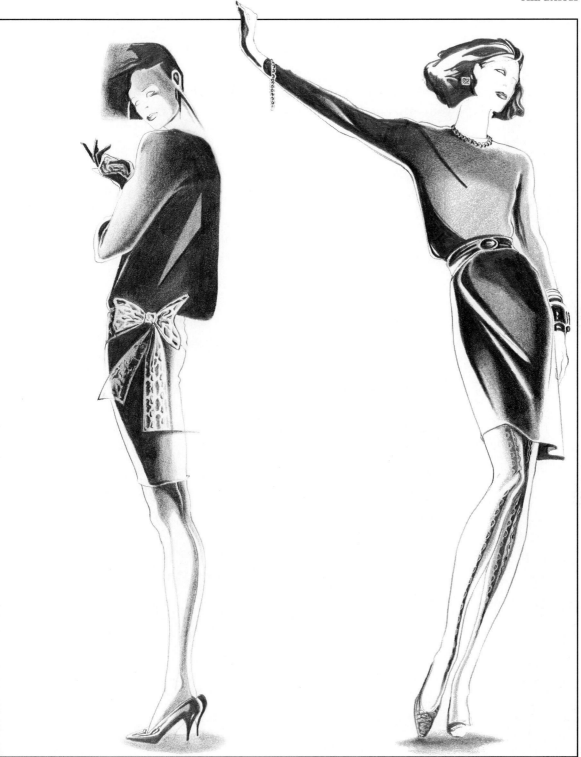

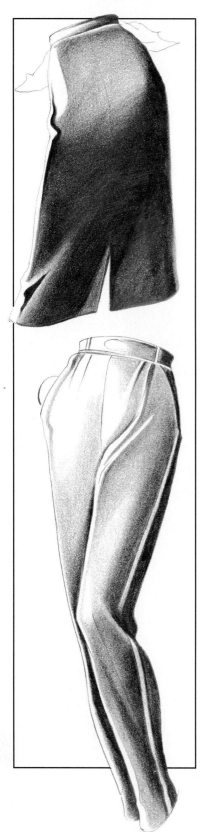

Or you don't have a basic black dress—not literally. You have, instead, *pieces* of black that you can put together as a dress or dress-equivalent—i.e., skirt and top, pants and top. And it's going to work just beautifully for you—provided you have the key pieces. If they coincide with the following, you're off and running.

A Day-length Black Skirt—instantly adaptable to any evening where a short dressy dress would be appropriate. Whether you buy the skirt as part of a suit or buy it separately or have it made up, you want it to be: (1) *straight-falling:* a more basic shape than an A-line or dirndl, easier to move around with different tops, and, unless your hips are exceptionally heavy, it looks sexier; (2) preferably with a little *slit* up the side or back or even up the front: sexy, of course, but also easier to move in—a slim wraparound skirt gives you the same effect; (3) *a great-looking material.* That silky-feeling wool gabardine that you see in men's tuxedos is perfect to start with. Or you might think about glacé leather or a very supple suede. These fabrics, being just a tiny bit lustrous, are almost unlimited as to when you wear them, as opposed to, say, satin, which is always extremely dressy, or a duller-textured wool, which usually isn't going to be dressy enough.

A Pair of Black Dress Pants—as basic as your black skirt and made of the same stuff. And worn with the same tops (see below) that you wear with the skirt. If I could own just one pair, it would be of the silky wool gabardine that I like. I would look for a pair that had a ribbon stripe down the sides, like men's dress pants. If I couldn't find them in the women's department, I'd buy dress pants in the men's. As a matter of fact, I'd probably go there first—I love the fit of men's pants. If you're slim hipped, they're *divine!* If I could have more than one pair, I'd go for crepe de chine, taffeta, charmeuse, glacé leather and the supplest suede.

An Evening-length Black Skirt—more intrinsically gala than what we've been talking about, but no less basic. To me, the most useful and delicious such skirt to own is, hands down, a simple black taffeta circle, held up with an elasticized waistband. It should be three-quarter length—known as ballerina length in the fifties, midi or maxi in the sixties, depending on whether it fell to the bottom of the calf or to somewhere around the top of the ankle.

Either length is fine. The whole look of the skirt—the small (certainly smaller-looking) waist and the luxurious splurge of taffeta, with a glimpse of a petticoat or two underneath, has got to be *the* most flattering proportion for a skirt ever invented! Add a pretty stocking and a pretty shoe (which could be a high-heeled sandal, or a charming little flat, à la Audrey Hepburn in *Sabrina*) and the look is perfect.

The easiest way to own one: make it yourself, or have someone make it for you. It isn't a very big deal, after all—a circle of taffeta made by stitching four half-circles together (see illustration) and joining seams at arrows, a piece of elastic, a hem—and it's going to cost a lot less than if you were to buy it at some pricey little boutique (if you could even find it to buy!). Spend the difference on a bunch of tulle or, even more luxurious, taffeta petticoats, and wear them one, two, or more at a time. As we all know, the taller and thinner you are, the more you can get away with—on the other hand, I know plenty of small *self-confident* women who can get away with anything!

Since taffeta petticoats are made the same way as the skirt, each petticoat equals one extra taffeta skirt, which opens up a sea of possibilities. Here's one to think about when you've got a big night ahead of you: put the red taffeta over the black, with lacy black stockings, high-heeled black satin sandals, plus long, crushed apple-green gloves—and your hair done up like a concierge's, with little wisps and tendrils curling around your face. Shades of Jane Avril. Adorable!

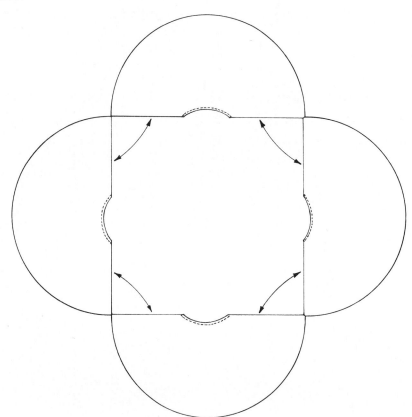

About long skirts: frankly, I have trouble with straight, floor-length black skirts, with no opening at the bottom. A plain black skirt to the floor and a blouse looks a bit frumpy and bourgeois to me.

If you're thinking of getting one because it will give you a long line, don't—pants will do it better. If you're thinking that longer is dressier, it isn't—length has very little to do with dressiness (except for the very biggest white-tie evenings, where you'd be wearing your ball gown).

But, okay. You already own this long, straight, unslit black skirt. Don't be too quick to chuck it out; especially don't if you happen to be tall and thin as a splinter. But do, for God's sake, give it a little pizzazz! Put a slit in it, first of all—a nice, long slash right up the side, so you've got some leg showing. Put a longish jacket with it—lamé or brocade, with a lot of jeweling or embroidery on top. Or use a plain black jacket with *big* shoulders (you want to pull the eye *up*, is the point) and fill in the neckline with ropes and strands and coils of necklaces.

Then put a belt on the jacket—a big, wide belt—and pull it in tight, which creates a small peplum and makes the line around the hips rather interesting. Now you've got a little something going for you. A little 1930ish something. You might even want to sweep up all your hair in a turban, or stick on a little velvet pancake of a hat. Not bad at all.

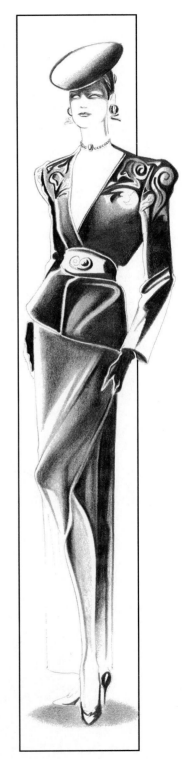

48

Basic Black Tops—of which you can't have too many. But if you're starting from scratch, the following are musts. A perfectly plain *black pullover,* long sleeved, crew necked or round necked, or oval necked (the less ribbing the better). Cashmere is ideal, but any soft, close-knit wool is fine, as is an angora blend. Cotton is the cashmere of summer; silk works all the time. A *silky, soft-collared black shirt*—crepe de chine, textury crepe, charmeuse, silk jersey, et al. (I'd scratch the classic silk broadcloth shirt with man-tailored collar—it's a little too prim and proper to be glamorous.) A frail little *black lingerie top* with slippy straps (which might be the top of a slip with skirts, the top of a "teddy" with pants—these days, thanks to the likes of such designers as Fernando Sanchez, you can find some of the most entrancing things to

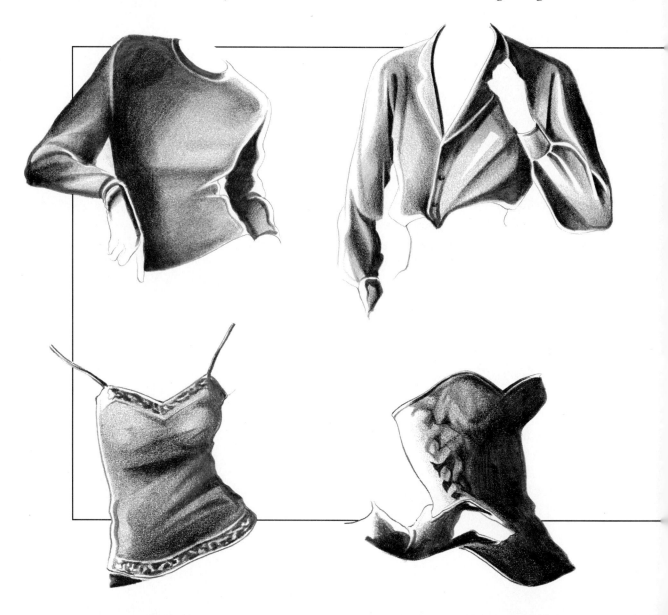

dress up in at almost any good lingerie shop). A bare, strapped, very *fitted black top like a little corset* (in taffeta or lace, and especially pretty to wear with three-quarter-length taffeta skirts). An *embroidered black sweater,* blazing with beads, sequins, appliqués, satin patches, metallic discs—as much jewel as sweater! An *embroidered black sweatshirt* (the less-dressy counterpart of the embroidered sweater). You can add the embroidery or jewels yourself. A lot of classic *black T-shirts,* and some embroidered ones, too.

All of the above, of course, are wonderful to have in colors. But the point about starting with black tops and black skirts and pants is that you have instantly the all-of-a-pieceness of a dress. The word is basic.

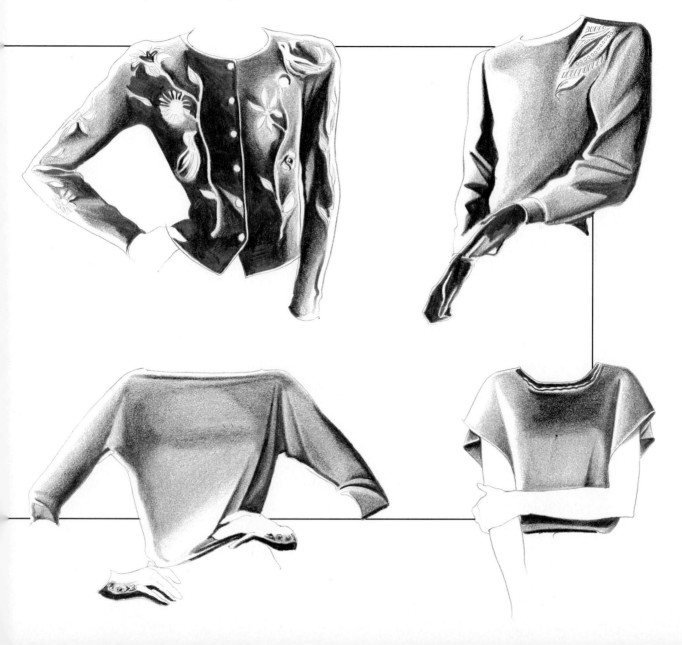

And of course to go with all of this basic black you must have the little black shoe. Actually, there are three styles that will round out your basic wardrobe nicely. They are:

The little black sandal. And it must be in satin. Many women think patent leather is dressy, but satin is dressier. By sandal, I mean an elegant shoe with lots of sexy little straps. This is the shoe that you can wear with any evening dress—whether you go long or short. And it can be a high heel or a low heel. But remember, the higher the heel the better. A high heel always flatters the leg.

Then there is the great-looking *classic black pump*—plain, beautiful and always appropriate. Patent leather is nice, but it is not as dressy as satin. For

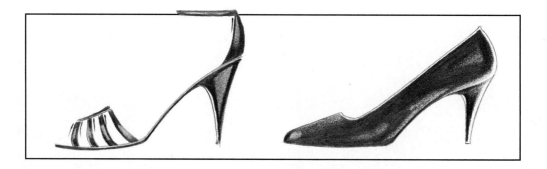

pants I prefer wearing *little flat pumps.* These can be in black patent leather, black lizard or some type of black skin. They are perfect with your black tuxedo pants and look great with dressed-up jeans.

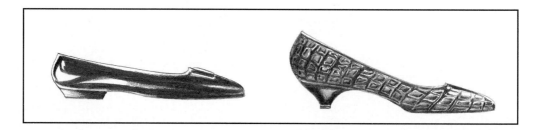

Now with all of this black you must have at least one *zinger* shoe—a brightly colored shoe (pink, red, green or whatever you love most) as a basic to perk up your black. It can have few straps or lots of straps, a high heel or a low heel. It can be sequined, beaded or whatever is pretty and fun. You can never have enough zingers in your wardrobe. This little zinger can be your starting point for accessorizing. So you have on your little black dress. You slip into your red zinger shoes and wrap your neck in wonderful red stones and rhinestone chains. Maybe you have a wonderful black jacket with flecks of red, gold and green running through it. Finish off with lots of gold bracelets and big chunky earrings before you pull on a pair of red leather gloves. Your little black dress has blossomed into a bright red poppy. And all because of those red zinger shoes.

You might want to include a little gold sandal or flat with your basics. Silver is nice too. These are as basic as black, but more dazzling to look at.

As for basic bags. You don't want to be carrying around one of those large day things. For dressing up, the smaller the better. And no straps. Just a little *black satin or velvet envelope-type bag* with a jeweled clasp. Or add your own jeweled brooch to it. A second basic bag could be in gold or silver. Maybe one of those little mesh bags. The bag I carry most often is a small, neat rectangle done in pleated black satin. Very basic and perfect for *anything.*

Now you've got it all except for your basic wrap. It is at this point of dressing up that many women panic. If you can afford it, by all means buy a great-looking fur coat. Find a coat that is suitable for day and night. A wonderful-looking brown sable, black mink or white lynx will do. *But you can look just as great without a fur.* With a little fabric and a little imagination you can create several basic wraps, all of them stunning. A little velvet stole that you can just throw around yourself is a very versatile wrap. This can be long or short. I have a velvet stole that I wear for very dressy and not-so-dressy occasions. It looks great with everything.

If you can't find one, nothing could be simpler to make. Take a large rectangular piece of velvet (or any dressy fabric) and line it with wool. Or with something interesting, like white satin or fur. Let's say you've got this sad old fur lying around. You can chop it up and use it as a lining and a trim around your stole.

Or try a big square of fabric folded over into a triangle. Wrap it around you and fasten it closed with a jeweled brooch. Or a circular piece of cashmere, with a hole in the middle and slit down the front, will wrap around you nicely. It's also easy to make an opera cape, as the illustration on page 54 shows.

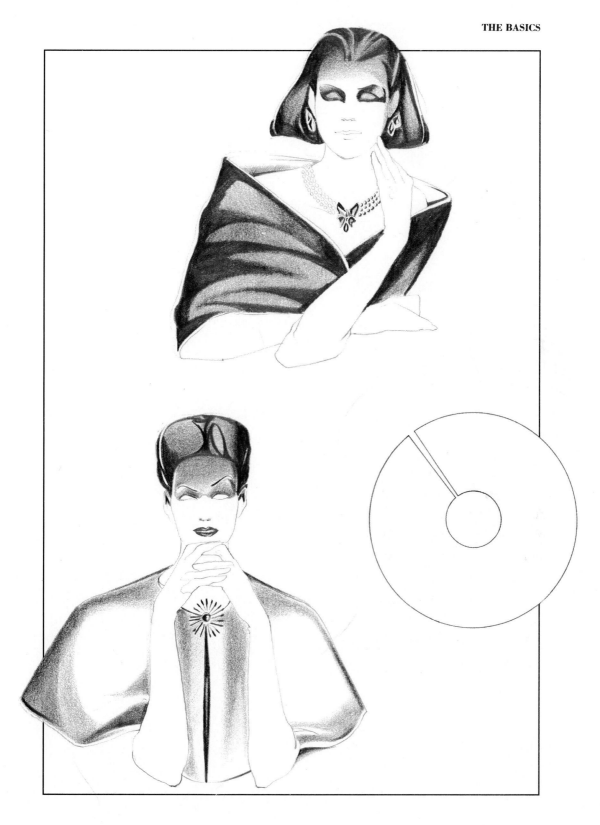

54

On the subject of basics, there's one more: blue jeans. For a certain kind of little evening—and with the tops already mentioned—they work like a dream. There are many different styles and kinds; go with those that make your bottom and legs look their best. You can dress up these jeans with:

- a sexy evening T-shirt, lots of jewels and high heels.
- a tuxedo jacket. It's done a lot, but it always looks good. And a pair of black patent-leather flats.
- jeweled or embroidered sweaters. Top with a little satin jacket and a pair of gold sandals.
- just a plain black or white T-shirt. Then pile on the necklaces, bracelets and a pair of big earrings. Add an interesting jacket.

I often go out to dinner in New York or Paris in just a pair of jeans, a little pair of flats and maybe an interesting jacket. I add great masses of necklaces and bracelets. With any of these combinations you have a definite look and can make any old tired pair of jeans look great.

3

ICING ON THE CAKE—PUTTING IT ALL TOGETHER

NOW. Tabula rasa. You've got your basics put together for dressing up, so you are halfway there. It's just a matter of mixing and matching and building your look with accessories. Accessories are what give you the dazzle. They're what dressing up is all about. You've got as many looks as you've got jackets, sweaters, shoes, scarves, jewels and color. Yes, lots of color. A real pastiche. All of it splashed everywhere. This is where the fun begins.

JEWELRY

I love the sound of clanking bracelets, the wonderful feeling of metal against my skin. Sensual. Luxurious. That's what jewelry does. It gives one a sense of luxury. And opulence. And glamour. The more you wear the better.

Most women are afraid of jewelry. I don't mean little necklaces and earrings that one can hardly see, I mean the big stuff. They think it will be overbearing or that they'll look too flashy. Or they think it won't suit them because they are too small, or too fat, or too whatever. Rubbish! They just don't dare.

Recently, while in Paris, I was asked to be on a panel of judges for a model-of-the-year contest. It was held at Castels—men in black tie and women

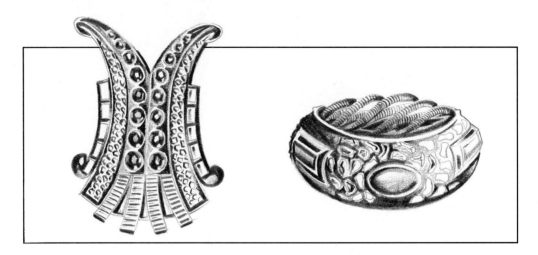

in short dressy. I was wearing a short black lace dress—very sexy. That afternoon a jeweler called me and asked if I would wear his jewels for the evening. When I went over to see the jeweler I was presented with two small gold, pearl and diamond necklaces and some tiny diamond earrings. Definitely not my cup of tea. And when I put them with the dress they just didn't do it. What I wore instead were wonderful enormous pieces that consisted of rhinestones, black jade and pearls all intertwined. And of course there were big earrings of the same. Now this jewelry *did it*. In this case bigger was definitely better than real.

You don't need real jewels to look great. A tiny diamond pendant and little diamond stud earrings, although real, are far less effective than some marvelous big fake piece that you put on. If you have beautiful real jewels, by all means, wear them. But for most of us, costume jewelry is the only way we can afford to go. (I often mix the fake with the real.) It's worth investing in good costume jewelry, because you can dress up *anything* with it—even your jeans. Most department stores carry an amazing selection in all price ranges. Even more fun are the little antique shops that specialize in thirties and fifties paste jewelry. Also if you travel look for interesting pieces wherever you go. Many times you can get very good prices on the real thing, too. For instance, in the Orient you will be able to find all kinds of real pearls, jades and corals—and for very little money. In Brazil you can get precious and semiprecious stones for practically nothing. Mexico is good for silver and Aruba, in the Caribbean, is good for gold.

Unless it's a special one-of-a-kind piece or a very large piece, always buy several of everything. Buy an armful of bracelets and a row of necklaces that

OPPOSITE: Vogue *modeling days, 1969. I loved lots of jewelry for dressing up.*

Vogue *modeling days. I say pearls are a girl's best friend.*

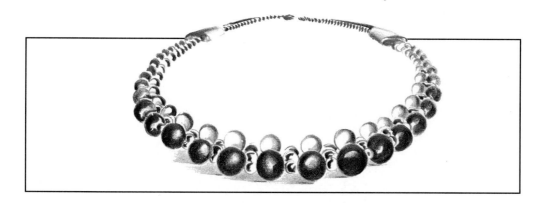

you can tier down your front. If you could buy only one jewel for your jewelry wardrobe, I'd say buy pearls. They go with *anything* and they are appropriate for *everything.* Pearls come by the strand (in all colors) and they come by the creation. And there are so many different ways to wear them. You can:

- ❦ wear them as a choker.
- ❦ wear them in strands, one after another in all different lengths and colors.
- ❦ wear one long strand knotted.
- ❦ wear a pearl necklace with a gorgeous jeweled clasp, but wear it so the jeweled clasp shows in the front.
- ❦ wear a choker with longer strands.

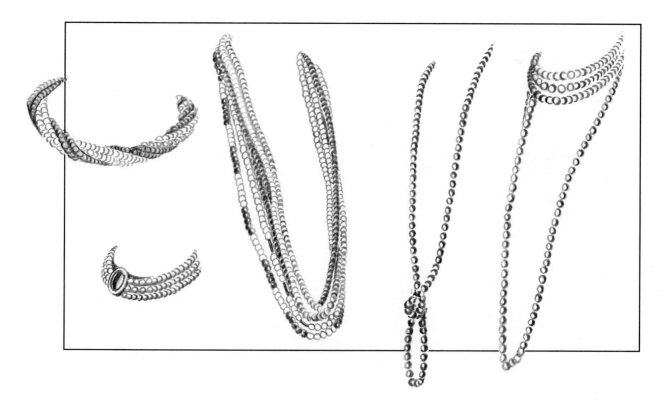

If you're starting from scratch buy:

- ❦ lots of pearls in different lengths and different colors: white, gray, black and pink.
- ❦ lots of rhinestones and crystals.
- ❦ chains: silver plated and gold filled are fine.
- ❦ all kinds of bangles: clunky, thin, chained, beaded and baubled.
- ❦ puffed bracelets: rhinestones, gold, pearls.
- ❦ big earrings: faux pearls, rhinestones, crystals, different colored stones, chunks of gold or silver (these can be either drop or clasp earrings).

Look for interesting designs. To this basic list you can add corals, jades, ivory, turquoise—whatever you like that suits your fancy.

Now that you've got it, put it on. When putting it on I always consider my neckline. In general you should choose pieces that follow, rather than cut, the contour of your neckline. Work with the neckline and follow the shape.

Be courageous and *really* put it on. But what's most important is that you feel confident as well as glamorous. If this is new to you start slowly and build your look gradually—two bracelets tonight, five tomorrow night. Maybe three

rows of pearls in different colors instead of just one. Experiment. One look tonight, another tomorrow night. Pearls with the jeans and black T-shirt. Rhinestones with the jeans and red T-shirt. But remember: you can't change overnight. It takes time and involves a lot of self-discovery. Be patient with yourself and don't be afraid of overdoing it—I find that most women don't wear enough jewelry.

To inspire your imagination, here are some daring looks that I love:

Put on a one-of-a-kind pearl piece. Add three strands of white pearls tiered and one strand of pink pearls doubled up. Large pearl earrings finish the look.

Don't hesitate to mix one kind of stone with another. I wear rows of amethysts with a couple of strands of pale jade. You might want to add jade earrings or large purple clasps.

Buy an armful of bracelets when you travel to exotic lands—how about an armful of tortoiseshell (wear as many as you can—they only cost a penny apiece) from Bali or South America, or ivory from Hong Kong?

One large, chunky coral and silver necklace is dressed up with strands and strands of smaller corals. To this I add silver cuffs studded with corals and

amber, or maybe some old silver bracelets. How about some large, interesting silver earrings?

With a large pair of earrings—lots of stones and lots of gold—and some stunning bracelets you can forget about your neckline. So wear your favorite ruffled silk shirt or one with a big bow that ties in the front. (I put a cuff on one arm and lots of gold bangles on the other.)

I love this look! Several silver and rhinestone bracelets one after the other up my arm, some fabulous cuffs with bright blue stones on my other arm, silver and rhinestone chokers. Finish the look with large silver earrings. This will turn any little black dress into a knockout.

I have two gold, diamond and purple-enamel necklaces. I add to these a couple of strands of midnight-blue pearls that have a heavy jeweled clasp. On goes a diamond cuff and big drop earrings made of gold and diamonds (they're really rhinestones, of course!).

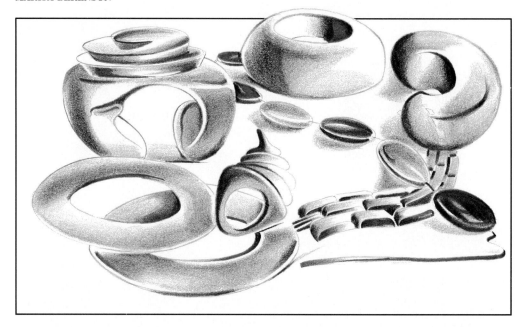

When you're building your jewelry wardrobe you might want to buy some fun pieces. I have a marvelous set of sculpted ivory bracelets and rings—*very large and very heavy.* It looks fantastic on a bare arm or with a very tight sleeve underneath.

Don't mix your basic chunky ethnic stones (turquoise, big pieces of coral, jade) with more refined stones (pearls and diamonds). For example, don't mix a large silver-and-turquoise Indian necklace with your little diamond and pearl strands.

You can turn a favorite necklace into a bracelet: just wrap it two or three times (depending on the length) around your wrist. You can do this with several necklaces and fill up your wrists.

If you have a bare back with a crew-neck front, try wearing your pearls down your back so that they are choker length in the front—it's fun and rather exotic looking!

Don't be afraid to wear just *one* earring, but make it a great one.

I have three pierced holes in one ear and just one pierced hole in the other, so sometimes I'll wear:

> ✻ a ruby, emerald and diamond in one ear and a big ruby in the other.
> ✻ a long earring made of pearls and rubies in one ear and a pearl, ruby and diamond in the other.
> ✻ a long earring in one ear and a long earring and two studs in the other.

Try a row of bracelets on a tight jersey sleeve. Or what about a pretty cuff over a ruffled sleeve? Wear the cuff above the ruffle.

Try wearing big jeweled clasp earrings places other than on your ears—on jacket lapels, pockets and collars.

It's fine to mix gold and silver—and a very good thing to do if you've got gold and silver sequins on your shoes, sweater, jacket or whatever.

If you're going with a certain period of jewelry, be consistent—don't mix the fifties paste with the turn-of-the-century antique.

Always mix your fake and real—no one will know the difference.

Use a toothbrush and toothpaste to clean your costume jewelry. Toothpaste really makes rhinestones sparkle.

When you're not wearing your pearls, leave them out. The more they "breathe," the more they'll shine. And the more you wear them, the more lustrous they'll get. They absorb the natural oils in your skin. Never spray perfume on your pearls—it will make them dull.

Jewelry size depends on your style, *not your size!* My grandmother was petite and always wore masses of jewelry. And big things—big brooches, bracelets, big rings. Lots of everything!

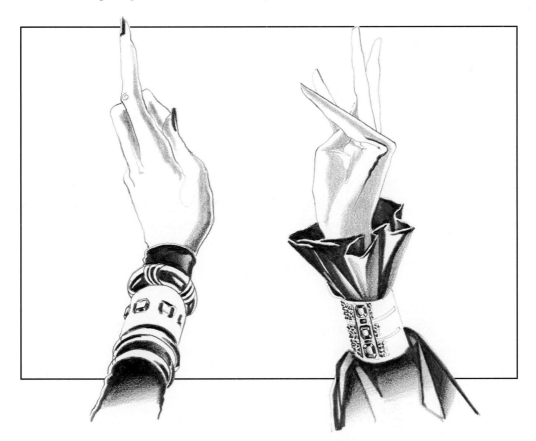

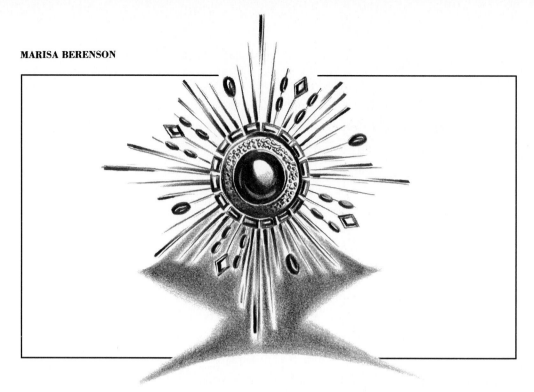

You've got it, you're wearing it, and you've got to take care of it. Costume jewelry has a tendency to fall apart if you don't take *good* care of it. I suggest that you invest in a small piece of furniture with lots of little drawers—like a cabinet—to keep your jewels in. It's much easier to keep track of what you've got, and it's the easiest way to keep everything sorted.

You can make or buy small fabric bags for storing your jewels. Plastic drawer dividers that you can find at the five-and-dime are good, too. Ideally, after you take your jewels off, you put them in their fabric bags or individual compartments of the drawer divider. Then store them in the cabinet drawers: bracelets in one drawer, earrings in another, etc. Put nails in the wall and you can hang each necklace.

I know that all of this takes time, but it's well worth it. Whatever you do, don't throw your jewelry all together in one lump. If you do, you'll find an impossible mess the next time you decide to wear any of it. There's nothing worse than being stuck on your bed with a pile of knotted-up necklaces, bracelets and brooches—especially when you could be out on the town having fun.

Tip: If you make the extra effort to look glamorous all of the time people will assume that you're wearing real jewels. The usual comment that I get when wearing my fabulous fakes is, "My God, Marisa, where did you get that marvelous piece?" I make up an interesting story and no one is the wiser!

COLOR   71

OH, GOD. I love color. Color is life. And warmth. And pizzazz. And exotic. And gay. Color is the world of possibilities when it comes to creating yourself and when it comes to dressing up. Next to jewelry, color is the most important accessory you have.

One has to be daring with color. Try wearing:

- a violet sweater with saffron-colored gloves and violet shoes. Finish the look with amber and coral around the neck, coral bracelets.
- bright red shoes with an electric-blue dress.
- turquoise sweater, red jewels, a wonderful red leather skirt.
- black pants, shocking-pink silk shirt. Wrap your waist in bright orange. Finish with orange, red or turquoise silk gloves.
- green and pink.
- navy with anything.
- black with anything.
- all shades of violet together, or pinks, reds, peaches, oranges.

Did you know that even the poorest women in India have a wonderful sense of color? They are wrapped and draped in the most fabulous colors. They mix bright pinks, oranges and yellows together. They even wear jewels: armfuls of skinny little bangles, ears dripping with gold. To walk through the streets of India and see these women is an inspiration.

When you dress up with color your energy level soars. Your total being is enhanced. So where do you begin and how do you do it? Well, there are no rules when you dress up with color. It depends entirely on you: colors might be determined by your complexion, your hair, your eyes, your personality. It's a matter of what you feel comfortable in and what suits you.

If you're planning a romantic evening *à deux,* you might want to try soft pinks, purples, mauves—of course they're marvelous in slinky, transparent fabrics. And I think red and black are always sexy, depending on what you are wearing—little silk pajamas, a dress cut to *here.*

Dressing up is a time for projecting yourself, creating an image. And you want to be bright and vivid. Yes, when in doubt grab black; it is your basic. But that doesn't mean if you go in a shop and see a great-looking pink or electric-blue dress that you shouldn't buy it. By all means do. And have fun with it.

72

At the end of the color section following Chapter 4 is a chart showing just a few of *my* favorite color combinations that you might want to try. Again, this will take some experimenting on your part to determine what you feel best in.

JACKETS

As far as I'm concerned the more jackets you have the better. You can dress anything up with them, and they pull your look together like *that*. Jackets are essential in my wardrobe. I say the more outrageous, beaded, embroidered, colorful and jeweled the better. The dressier the jacket, the more dressed up you'll look. And they are appropriate for *any* evening, depending on their degree of dressiness. You might want to consider the following:

- ✄ Add a heavily jeweled jacket to your little black dress and you are dressed for *black tie*. Add a plain, short, fitted, black satin or velvet jacket (with wonderful sleeves—puffed or padded) to your long black skirt. Go to town with the jewels and you will look stunning, even at *white-tie* occasions.
- ✄ Or add a heavily jeweled jacket to that long black skirt for *white tie*.
- ✄ As stated before, a tuxedo jacket will really dress up a pair of jeans for a night on the town. (Lots of jewels, of course!)
- ✄ Add a sequined or lace tailored jacket to a short black skirt for cocktail parties.

You can experiment with all lengths, but remember that a short, fitted jacket works with anything. Sometimes when I find interesting buttons I add them to a jacket. The more original the better—old buttons, buttons with strange faces, animal buttons, jeweled buttons. You can be as creative as you want. Why not sew some rhinestones on a plain black jacket, or add red jeweled buttons to that little black velvet number you found recently?

Apart from the usual stores try thrift shops for thirties boleros, men's smoking jackets, Edwardian combing jackets. If you're in New York City, go to Chinatown for quilted jackets and SoHo for patchwork jackets in ravishing silks. And of course, there's always your mother's closet. My own most-treasured-of-all jackets belonged to my grandmother. I've been wearing

them for the last fifteen years, and they weren't new to begin with—*the* most divine hand-me-downs anyone could wish for! Remember: nothing is too old or unusual to wear.

SWEATERS

A jeweled sweater is not as dressy as a jeweled jacket and should not be thought of as a substitute. Think of it as a casual way of dressing up. It's great for cocktail parties or a night on the town when put with a short skirt, a pair of black dress pants or a pair of blue jeans. (By the way, jeweled sweaters are also great to wear during the day.)

Along the same line as jeweled sweaters are embroidered sweaters, pearled sweaters, sequined sweaters and sweaters with ribbons—all great for dressing up in. Look for interesting designs and styles: padded shoulders, puffed sleeves or décolleté. Little sweaters and big sweaters—sweaters so big that they could be a tunic over pants or a dress all by themselves.

Instead of wearing a silk shirt (it can get rather boring), try a jeweled sweater over your black dress pants. Step into a pair of gold or silver flats—or maybe flats the color of one of the jewels. Add some great earrings (again picking up colors in the sweater) and bracelets. What kind and how many bracelets you wear will depend on the sleeve—is it heavily jeweled or plain? If it's got a lot on it, simple bangles are your best bet. What do you do with your neckline? Nothing! If the sweater is really dazzling let it speak for itself. There's no need for beads and chains—it's all *going on* right there on the sweater.

SCARVES

I'm not particularly keen on scarves. But I say if you're going to wear one, really do something with it. Don't just leave it hanging. You can:

- wrap one around your waist.
- tie one in a big floppy bow around your neck.
- use small, thin metallic ones as hair ribbons.
- wrap a long glittery scarf around your wrist several times and knot it.
- use a brightly colored scarf as a choker by twisting it, wrapping it tightly around your neck a few times and knotting it.
- in the summer experiment with extra-large scarves as wraps and shawls.
- wrap your head turban-style with a pretty scarf.

I use scarves more as a final wrapping—big, wonderful scarves that you can throw over yourself or around yourself. I might just throw a big one over my shoulder before going out the door. Or use one as a final wrapping around my evening coat—keeping it in place with a big jeweled brooch, of course!

And nothing could be simpler to make; just buy some dazzling cloth and put a hem around it. (I have a few large pieces of brocade and gold fabric that I wear as scarves.) So if you do favor wearing scarves, go with something bright and metallic or big and jazzy. And by all means do something with them, because they *can* be so boring.

76   *SHOES AND BELTS*

A pair of exotic shoes or a spectacular belt can turn your basic black from dull to dazzling. And it is possible with either to be outrageous without feeling overdone.

For instance, one can have a real adventure with an unusual pair of shoes. Let's say that you find a pair of lavender silk sandals with the strippiest straps and four-inch heels, but you don't have a matching dress. Buy them anyway—they're going to be much more seductive with your black things. (If you want to match the sandals, do so with a stocking—although a sheer black stocking is sexy all of the time.) And when you go through your jewels, maybe you'll find some earrings with a lovely purple stone, or you'll see the color in the beads of a necklace. Maybe you'll want to turban your head with a gorgeous scarf, and you'll see a hint of the same lavender in the fabric. Before you know it, those lavender sandals have created a whole look.

When I say dress up with a belt, I don't mean a little belt—I mean something big, outspoken and glorious. How about a big band of satin cinching your waist tiny, topped off with a big rhinestone buckle? Or strands and strands of silken cord in all different colors intertwined, with big pom-poms on the ends, that you wrap around your waist several times? You can pick up one of the colors with your shoes and gloves.

The point is that almost anything is possible when it comes to belts and shoes (like metallic red boots under black silk pants) and almost everything is available. Look for a variety of textures, colors and designs when you

shop—and have fun! Creative dressing up with belts and shoes gives you a chance to try out the newest fads while making use of your basic black.

GLOVES

A brief word about them. Back in the "old days" no woman would go out without her gloves. They were a symbol of her femininity, and they showed she was a lady. I think gloves are marvelous because they're the perfect finishing touch. Just imagine—you have it all on and you put on a wonderful pair of evening gloves: satin, taffeta, sequined, soft kid. Long, short, or somewhere in between. They make you look pulled together and chic. It's the gloves that give you that touch of pizzazz.

When you accessorize with gloves there are no rules; it's really a question of personal taste and what you think suits you best. It's preferable that they pick up a color you are already wearing. But that doesn't mean that if you've found a splendid electric-blue cocktail dress that you shouldn't wear your ruby satin gloves—by all means do. And while you're at it why not add that chunky ruby rhinestone necklace, bracelets and big drop earrings—bold but seductive. Speaking of seductive, I think there's something very seductive about a woman peeling off a tight pair of gloves. Now that's something to think about. I adore wearing gloves—thank God they're coming back!

There are lots of possibilities with your separates. Watch me build two dazzling looks with a basic tuxedo and lots of separates.

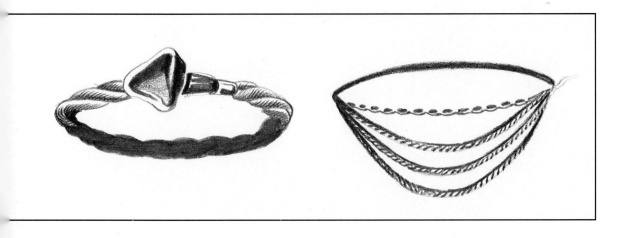

THE TUXEDO LOOK. STUNNING. PERFECT FOR ANY LITTLE EVENING:
A CHIC DINNER, COCKTAILS, THEATER OR A NIGHT ON THE TOWN, TO NAME JUST A FEW

I put on some wonderful lace stockings but skip the bra.

I add a crepe de chine jacquard blouse in a lively fuchsia color. Now for the tuxedo pants and a black leather belt with an exotic jeweled buckle. Why not coordinate the blouse with fuchsia-colored leather pumps?

Strands and strands of pearls with big jeweled clasps look wonderful. And why not add big pearl earrings and pearl cuff bracelets?

Add a short black jacket with satin lapels to finish the look. I pull up the ruffled collar of my blouse so that it's outside the lapels and frames my face. I carry the perfect black satin envelope bag.

PARTY DRESS. EXTRAVAGANT AND LOTS OF FUN.
THIS IS A REAL PARTY DRESS APPROPRIATE FOR SEMIFORMAL, DANCING AND GENERAL
CARRYING ON!

82

First some of my favorites: garters, panties, turquoise stockings and a red satin bustier top. My red suede pumps have bugle beads and sequins for that extra dazzle.

Now I put on tulle and satin petticoats, with lots of colors. Here I add a red tulle and then purple and acid-green satin.

Now for the black taffeta skirt—stunning over all of those petticoats! I sash the whole look with a band of purple corded fabric.

For the finishing touch I put on three-quarter length purple satin gloves (a treasure from Grandmother) and a fun, colorful crystal and cut-glass cuff. No necklace—just big earrings that match the cuff. I wrap myself in tulle for a show, and I'm ready for the night. Question is, is the night ready for me?

4

DRESS REHEARSAL

A BIG PART of dressing up is being prepared for it. This means having the right clothes at the right time that are right for you. It's almost impossible to be anxious about dressing up when you know that you've got great-looking clothes hanging neatly in your closet with the right accessories that will have you dressed up in a pinch. To exist, this state of grace involves a little "homework." You must know what styles look best on you, be a smart shopper, and know how to take care of your clothes.

HOW TO MAKE THE MOST OF WHAT YOU'VE GOT

The fashion ideal is a long, slim look. Unfortunately for most of us it's more of a wish than a reality. We spend half our lives either taking off the excess or filling in the gaps. I don't know one woman who is totally happy with her body—there's either too much of this or not enough of that.

I say, value the things that are best in yourself and *make the most of what you've got*. What good does it do to dwell on the negative? Instead, play up your assets and play down your figure flaws. If you are honest with yourself, and then shop accordingly, you can be confident that you'll always look terrific when you get dressed up.

Now for the hardest part. Get in front of a full-length mirror (if you don't have one, get one—preferably with a triple view—or you'll never know what you really look like), stripped, and be as objective as you can be. It could be that your waist is not as long and slim as you wish it were, but maybe you've got great-looking legs. Or your breasts aren't as large as you'd like them to be—but just think of all the things you can get away with: a décolleté to *here,* that little nothing evening top. The point is, really know your body and then dress accordingly. You'll have a better look and feel more confident dressed up because what you have on will suit you.

I can remember going to a friend's in Paris for a very chic party that included a formal sit-down dinner. It was a year when everyone was dressing bare. A good friend of mine from Germany was there, looking sexy and gorgeous as ever. She was wearing a dress cut in a long, low slinky V. Unfortunately, as she leaned forward to sip her soup, out popped her bosom into the bowl. Poor thing—she didn't know whether to laugh or cry as she fled the room. I know it's tempting to dress in the latest fads, but don't if it doesn't suit you.

There are lots of ways to camouflage your figure flaws. The most obvious way is to avoid wearing anything that attracts attention to a problem area. Again, total honesty is necessary. If you are clever enough, only you will be aware that you have any figure faults at all. The following tricks, depending on your problem, will help give you a long, slim look.

SHORT WAIST
- Avoid wide waistbands and wide belts. Narrow waistbands and narrow belts give the illusion of one long, fluid line.
- Try wearing belts a little below the waist.
- Don't tuck pullover tops in. Wearing them over skirts or pants keeps the waist undefined and gives the illusion of length.
- Wear matching or toned tops and bottoms.

WIDE HIPS AND LARGE THIGHS
- Avoid clingy fabrics and horizontal patterns.
- Trouser-pleated skirts and pants only add emphasis—why not try slightly gathered, narrow skirts instead?
- Cinching the waist with a wide belt will make your hips look *wider,* so stick with narrow belts.
- Simplicity is best. Too many pleats, back zippers, back pockets (especially on jeans) and gathers attract the eye like arrows.

BIG BOSOM

❧ Don't wear double-breasted coats or jackets.

❧ Avoid anything that's too detailed or fussy on top. Ruffles, breast pockets and big buttons will make you look bigger.

❧ Be careful with necklines that are very low and revealing.

❧ Wearing open-necked sweaters, blouses and dresses will create a vertical line, giving the illusion of a long, lean line.

NARROW SHOULDERS

❧ Try shoulder pads in jackets and tops. Horizontal patterns and epaulets will also give an illusion of width.

BROAD SHOULDERS

❧ Remove shoulder pads from your clothes and avoid horizontal seams and lines.

❧ Raglan sleeves are always good to wear because they pull the eye down from the shoulder.

BULGING STOMACH

❧ Stay away from anything that cinches your waist—it will only accent your stomach.

❧ Keep your pants and skirts loose so that the fabric doesn't bind or pucker.

❧ Wear skirts with gentle side gathers or side pockets. They draw the eye away from the bulge.

SHORT LEGS

❧ Avoid cuffed pants.

❧ The more delicate the shoe and the higher the heel, the better.

❧ Avoid ankle-length pants, midcalf skirts and ankle-strap shoes.

❧ A slit up the front of the skirt showing a little bit of leg gives the illusion of length.

TIPS TO MAKE ANYONE LOOK SLIMMER

❧ Wraparound skirts are always flattering.

❧ Open necklines in a V always give the illusion of a longer look.

❧ A tiny bit of shoulder padding can give you a lift and a longer, slimmer line.

❧ Soft, graceful fabrics that move with the body are best: wool, jersey, silk, cotton gabardine. Remember that stiff, heavy fabrics make you look bulkier.

❧ Don't be afraid to show your back. A bare back can be sexy at any age.

Remember, while a woman with a less-than-perfect body needs to play down her imperfections, for every imperfection there is another marvelous quality that makes up for it. A dazzling smile and glowing hair are just as important as a tiny waist and a beautiful bosom. So what if your legs aren't long and slender. Maybe you have a beautiful neckline instead. By all means, show it off!

SHOPPING TIPS

While the idea of *Dressing Up* is to show you how to dress up without the panicked feeling that you have to rush out and buy something new, I must confess that I love to shop. What could be more wonderful than browsing leisurely and buying on a whim? When I see something I like, I buy it. I never question whether I have something to wear with it because I know eventually I'll work it into my wardrobe. If you see something you love, but it's not what you're shopping for specifically, I say buy it if you can afford it. Believe me, you'll figure out a way to use it.

But that's all *fun* shopping—I'm sure we all know how to do that. What's difficult is shopping for the things that count. Especially when you have a tight budget to stay within.

The first thing I recommend is that you buy separates (refer back to Chapter 2). This way you can mix and match and have several outfits instead of just two or three. What woman doesn't get bored with her clothes? When you work with your separates you have a greater variety in your wardrobe.

Evaluate your wardrobe and see what you really need. It's always best to know what you're looking for when you go shopping. You'll save yourself a good deal of time and possibly hours of frustration. Just imagine going through rack after rack, not knowing whether you want a skirt or a pair of dress pants.

Look for quality clothing when you shop. You'll get a lot more wear out of one beautiful black cashmere sweater than two less-expensive synthetic blends. A cashmere sweater is classic, is always appropriate and can always be dressed up. You should also be wary of sales or bargains. Oftentimes the merchandise is flawed in one way or another. A bargain is a waste of money if it's too flawed to wear.

But that is not to say you should pass up boutique or designer sales at the

This is a great "little black dress"—as stylish then as it is now. See the color section for an updated version.

end of the season. You might just find that perfect finishing touch—maybe that wonderful beaded jacket you normally couldn't afford. Just remember to check the garment carefully before you buy it.

Think of clothing as an investment and remember that a "good" investment will last years and continue to look good. I have things in my wardrobe that I've worn twenty years.

94

Ask yourself the following questions before you buy:

- Is the garment well cut?
- Is the garment well proportioned?
- Is the garment made out of quality fabric that will wear well?
- Does the garment suit your body?
- And most important of all, *how do you feel in it?* You should feel comfortable and confident in whatever you buy. Clothing should make you feel good and delight you at all times. Nothing looks worse or makes you feel worse than poorly made clothing that hangs improperly or rides up the body.

TAKING CARE OF YOUR CLOTHES

My ultimate fantasy is to have a "closet" room where all my clothes can be properly kept and maintained. What could be more wonderful than a roomful of racks, shelves and special compartments for every belt, pair of gloves, pair of shoes and hat? Unfortunately, for most of us, there is never enough closet space. At times, who hasn't been tempted just to throw things in? But what's the point of having beautiful things if they are wrinkled and mussed when you go to wear them? The sense of panic can be overwhelming when you've planned on that little silk chemise for the evening, and then find it in a ball on the closet floor. And let's face it, the better you take care of your clothes, the longer they'll last. Since you're apt to use your business and sports wardrobes more heavily, your dressy clothing probably gets scrunched at the back of the closet. These nuts-and-bolts tips on maintaining your elegant attire should make dressing up easier, as your clothes will always be ready for you:

- Hang like things together: for instance, keep all the shirts together, the pants, the jackets, etc. Specific garments will be a lot easier to find.
- When you hang up a coat or jacket, make sure you button it completely and that the collar and lapels are lying straight. Now check the shoulders to make sure they sit straight across the hanger—this way the coat will fall properly and maintain its shape.
- Throw out those awful wire hangers and invest in the padded-fabric types. Blouses and dresses will stay fresh looking and hold their shape.
- Use tissue paper under the clips of your skirt hangers—this is essential for velvets and leather.

❀ Hold onto the plastic bags and tissue paper that come back with the dry cleaning. Both are perfect for protecting your clothes. Dry-cleaning bags may be used to cover dresses and blouses. Use the tissue paper over hangers before you hang your pants. This keeps them from creasing.

❀ You should invest in good garment bags for your more fragile pieces.

❀ Hang porcelain pomanders along with your favorite garments to keep your clothing fresh and fragrant.

❀ I keep all my delicates in plastic bags or cloth pouches—nightgowns in one, panties in another, hose in another, etc. This way they're easy to keep track of and easy to pack for a trip. Of course, I slip a sweet-smelling sachet in each pouch.

❀ To keep your shoes fresh looking put tissue paper in the toes.

❀ Scarves, gloves, hats and belts can be kept separately in small fabric bags. This way they're never scattered—what could be worse than having only one yellow glove?

DRESS REHEARSAL

At *Vogue,* nothing goes to the photographer's studio until it's been totally rehearsed with jewelry, scarves, bags, etc. You'd be surprised how much last-minute panic is avoided. And it works just as well at home: once you've assembled your basic wardrobe, take the time to try the pieces in various combinations until you find the look that strikes your fancy for a particular social engagement.

By doing this you'll know exactly everything you have for that sort of occasion, and that your clothes are in tip-top shape—no scuffed shoes, torn hems, missing buttons, stains or wrinkles. Dress rehearsal gives you a chance to play and experiment with what you have to create a spectacular look.

Recently I had a dinner date with an old friend, whom I hadn't seen in years. "Oh, goodness," I thought, when I got out of bed that day, "what am I going to wear tonight?" There was nothing that I could think of that was particularly inspiring, but I wanted to make an impression because this was a very "special" friend. So I did what I always do in a case like this:

First, I went through my racks and pulled out a number of different black separates.

Then I got out every great-looking jacket I have, lots of different colored shoes and my favorite jewelry. I decided that I wanted to wear wonderful shocking-pink pumps with little cutouts in the toe. Once I had decided on the shocking-pink shoes, I went for a jacket that I had made from fabric I got in Hong Kong: a marvelous gold brocade with shocking pink, purple and green Chinese motifs throughout the fabric.

The shoes and the jacket gave me my "look," and to them I added a black taffeta skirt and a plain black sweater. I belted the jacket with a shocking-pink and black belt. I added lots of gold necklaces, black pearls and huge pink enamel earrings.

When my friend and I met later the first words out of his mouth were, "Marisa! Where did you get that fabulous outfit?" Little did he know that everything I had on was at least ten years old—except for the shoes. My dress rehearsal had paid off, and all it took was fifteen minutes!

Once you've dress rehearsed your look for the evening, you're free to relax and enjoy the ritual to come. Any great night out starts with a few quiet moments to pamper yourself.

Dressed up for a gala evening—the most elegant of occasions.

A black-tie night—an evening to remember.

OPPOSITE: This little black dress has been around for years and could go anywhere!

This little black skirt and jacket are perfect for theater,
dinner, cocktails—any little night on the town.

OPPOSITE: *My favorite party dress.*

The tuxedo look is my favorite choice when I don't know what to wear for a little evening.

A VARIETY OF EVENING MAKEUP AND HAIR LOOKS

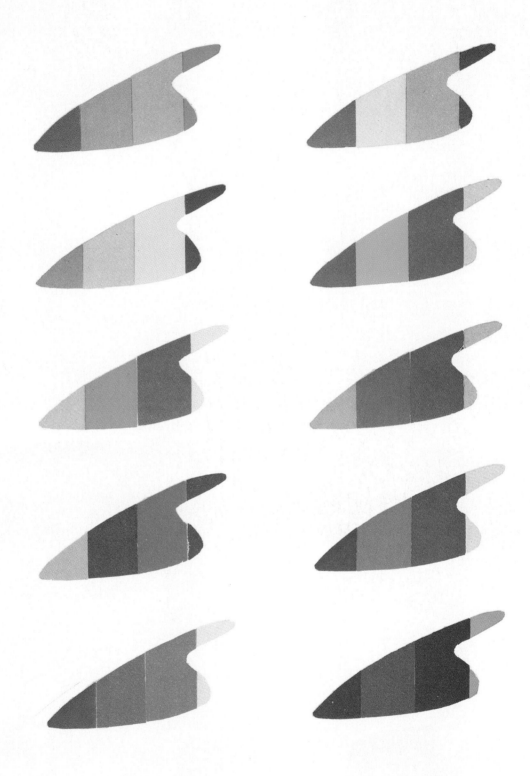

Here are some daring color combinations that might not occur to you. These are just a few of my favorites. Try two or all four in each group—the balance is up to you.

THE RITUAL

THE HOUR OR TWO you spend alone, preparing for the evening to come, is a very important time. Your toilette should be luxuriously sensual and should heighten your anticipation of the evening ahead. You relax, primp, pluck, peel and soak—whatever is necessary to prepare your body and face for the wonderful clothes, jewels and makeup to come. At the same time, you are stripping away accumulated layers of tension and stress. As you do so, you are creating the confidence, poise and mood you wish to project that night. For as important as good grooming is to dressing up, fantasy, vitality and a sense of fun are what will make you memorably radiant.

Each woman has her own ritual—those little things she does to revitalize and bring herself up to her highest energy level. For me its *Bath Beautiful, Mask Marvelous, Constructive Lie-down* and a big *whoosh* of some *Fabulous Fragrance.* In just one short hour I am revitalized and ready for anything!

Let the ritual begin . . .

BATH BEAUTIFUL

The first step in the ritual is a restoring, herbal bath. Let's consider the bathroom. No matter how large or how small your bathroom is, it is your private sanctuary. It is your place to unwind, relax and escape as you prepare for the big evening ahead. If you want your bath time to be the ultimate pleasure that it should be, you need to equip your bathroom with some essentials:

- ❧ as many candles as you like (Either scented or unscented are fine.)
- ❧ a cassette recorder and a stack of your favorite cassettes (I'd have several kinds, because you never know what your mood will be or how it will change once you start to relax.)
- ❧ incense that you can burn
- ❧ scented soap that matches your perfume
- ❧ big fluffy bath towels to wrap yourself in
- ❧ a nice fluffy bath rug
- ❧ a favorite robe or kimono that you can slip into after your bath

And for the bath itself you will need:

- ❧ a selection of herbs to suit your bathing needs (A detailed description of my favorite herbs follows.)
- ❧ a plastic cushion or pillow for your head
- ❧ a loofah for sloughing off rough, dead skin
- ❧ a pumice stone for softening the soles of the feet, the elbows and knees
- ❧ a natural sea sponge

HEAVENLY HERBS

When I bathe, I *never* use bubble bath. It's very drying to the skin and can cause vaginal infections. Just think of the chemicals involved to make it bubble! What I do use are herbs. You can use them in any form, dry, or in oil base. Your bathwater will release their essences. Many health food stores or bath shops carry them already prepared to pour into the tub. You can also take them from your spice rack in their dried form and throw a handful into the bathwater. Or you can boil dried herbs ahead of time, straining and keeping the extract refrigerated until you are ready to pour some into your bath. Use as much as you like—until the bath is permeated with fragrance. If you use herbs in dried form, you may want to buy in bulk. My favorites are:

Rosemary—for waking up the system. Rosemary has long been used to invigorate the system. The rosemary wreath symbolized energy to the

Romans. When bathing in rosemary take a hotter bath for a shorter period of time.

Juniper Berry—for soothing tired muscles. The Romans used juniper berries to ward off evil spirits. When combined with wintergreen oil, it's the perfect bath to relieve aching muscles—especially after exercise. Bathe in juniper as you normally would.

Spruce and Pine Oil—lifts the spirits. When I'm depressed, nothing is better, and I feel as if I've stepped into a beautiful forest as I soak. These oils are the perfect skin softeners, so the longer you can soak the better.

Camomile—a gentle bath for stressed skin. This bath is particularly good if your skin has been exposed to too much sun or wind. Again, the longer you soak the better, and the bathwater shouldn't be too hot.

Thyme, Peppermint, Caraway and Sage (oils)—a pickup after work. Try these oils together in a very hot tub and feel yourself come alive. And there's a marvelous tingling that lingers afterward.

You might also want to try lavender, rose petals or lemon verbena. I could go on and on. The point is that there are all kinds of herbs, essences and oils available. Experiment and find what works best for you.

Tip: Feeling as if you're about to swoon from the heat? Try a hot bath with peppermint oil. Nothing cools you faster and it's great after a long day with an even longer evening to come.

Now, having assembled your grooming equipment and selected your herbal treat, you are ready to begin. Your bathroom has been transformed into your own personal spa. Off go the clothes and on goes the kimono. If you plan to wash your hair, do so now and wrap it in a fluffy towel. Then draw your bath—its temperature will depend on the herb or herbs you choose to use. While the tub is filling, set the mood: light the candles and turn off the lights. Put on a cassette that you're in the mood for and light the incense.

Now is a good time to condition your hair if you've washed it, or an oversized shower cap will protect your hair if you've had it professionally styled. Wash your face and slather on an extra-rich face cream—one that has collagen or elastin is best. Honey is good for around the delicate eye area, since it is a super moisturizer. By the time you have done all of this your bath should be ready.

Slip into that delicious, warm water. What could be more soothing or relaxing? I always say that a hot bath is a little bit of heaven. As you soak, not only is the tension leaving your body, but your face is getting a special moisturizing treatment. The steam and heat of the bath open the pores, allowing the moisturizer to penetrate beneath the skin's surface. Your whole body is breathing and relaxing.

You may want to have a favorite drink tubside—why not a little champagne or a glass of white wine to get you in the party spirit? This might be just what you need if you've had a particularly awful day. Or, if you're planning to dance all night, your favorite energizer might do the trick. I like fresh fruit juices or vegetable purees. Carrot juice with a little brewer's yeast is very uplifting—just think of all that vitamin B! And I find a nice cup of camomile tea soothing.

Before you begin washing, spend your first five minutes in the tub just lying back and relaxing. This is when you'll want to use the plastic cushion or pillow under your head. As you close your eyes, release all negative thoughts and let your mind just float. For your bath to really revitalize you, these five minutes of pure relaxation are crucial—especially if you don't have time for my Constructive Lie-down.

Five minutes and a few sips of champagne later you're ready to begin. The pumice stone is perfect for breaking down calluses and softening rough elbows and knees.

Use the loofah lightly to massage and stimulate your body—always massage toward the heart, moving the loofah in small circular motions. Wait until you see how this leaves the body glowing and the skin toned. A loofah massage is one of the best ways to slough off the dead cells that collect on the skin's surface. Finish with a light all-over washing with a natural sea sponge.

Many women include shaving as a part of their ritual, and the bath seems like the perfect place to do it. I say don't. If you do shave, chances are good that you'll cut yourself at least once and you could develop some nasty shaving rashes. And I don't like depilatories either because they're hard on the skin and can also give you rashes.

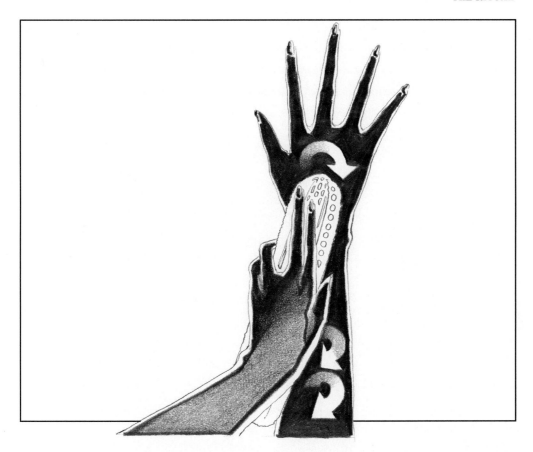

Have your legs and underarms waxed instead. It costs very little to have done and will last you almost a month. Each time you're waxed, a little less hair grows back. There are salons that specialize in waxing, and many hairdressers offer the service as well. Waxing has become as common as having a manicure.

Best of all, waxing leaves you with a smoother look. When you're dressing up you want a satin-smooth leg and underarm—there's nothing worse than having the nubs poke through your expensive stockings! Give your razor to your husband or lover.

A wonderful way to finish your bath, if you're brave, is with an ice-cold shower. If you've been conditioning your hair while bathing, start with a warm shower to get the conditioner out. Now on with the cold—as cold as you can stand it. The benefits are many: it closes the pores, gives your skin a rosy glow, and nothing makes your hair shine more than a rinse of ice-cold water.

Wrap yourself in one of your nice, big, fluffy bath towels—but only for a moment because you always want to apply your body lotion while the skin is moist. The body lotion will penetrate more if the skin is left moist.

MASK MARVELOUS

A mask does several wonderful things for your face. First it improves circulation, giving you a better color as it evens out splotchy skin. It also sloughs off dead surface cells, tightens enlarged pores and opens up clogged ones. What could be better?

There are hundreds of commercially made masks available for every skin type. If you buy your masks at a cosmetic counter look for masks with natural ingredients. And remember: a peeling mask sloughs off dead cells, a hydrating mask moisturizes, a nourishing mask revitalizes the face. Clay is also a good all-round mask, as it deep cleans and is rich in minerals.

My favorite mask is an *Aloe vera*-seaweed mask that I get from my skin specialist, Arsi, in New York. (You can write to her for a catalogue of all her natural products at Arsi Ltd., 14 East 60th Street, New York, NY 10022.) The healing qualities of the *Aloe vera* and the minerals in the seaweed penetrate to the fourth layer of the skin to create a smoother look.

After I use the *Aloe vera*-seaweed mask I feel as if my skin is literally breathing. And my skin looks and feels fabulous. This is what any good mask should do.

You don't necessarily have to buy a mask to have the same results. Chances are, you have appropriate ingredients right in your kitchen. Why not try:

Eggs. For an exhilarating facial, beat two raw eggs and apply them to your face. As the eggs dry, your face will feel stiff. Rinse with warm water. Finish by wiping your face with cucumber slices. (Cucumbers are great skin softeners.)

Milk. This one is as simple as choosing the right milk for your skin type: oily skin—skim milk, normal skin—homogenized milk, dry skin—cream. Apply, leave on until dry and rinse with cold water.

Brewer's Yeast and Honey. This combination is great for oily or acned skin. Just mix one tablespoon of brewer's yeast and a little honey—it should be a paste consistency. Apply, let dry and rinse.

Yogurt. Plain yogurt is another great facial—just slather it on, let it dry and rinse it off. Plain yogurt is also a perfect milky cleanser. Just work it into your skin and rinse it off.

HOW TO APPLY A MASK

To get the full benefit from your mask, you should learn how to apply it properly.

1. Wrap your hair in a towel or plastic so that it doesn't get in the mask. This is also a good time to condition your hair—while the mask dries, the conditioner works in your hair. Then you can remove it all at once in the shower.

2. Prime your face for the mask by taking a hot bath, applying a warm washcloth, or steaming your face (you can do this over a pan of *hot* water) to open your pores.

3. Now mix and apply your mask. *Always apply the mask in an upward direction.* Work from the neck, to the chin, around the cheeks, now the nose, up around the temples and across the forehead. *Avoid the eye area.*

4. You can use the time while waiting for the mask to dry to give yourself a manicure. Or try my Constructive Lie-down.

5. After fifteen–twenty minutes remove the mask. Rinse your face with warm water, then cool water, then cold. This way you gradually close the pores. You may want to finish off with witch hazel.

6. Apply a mask at least once a week.

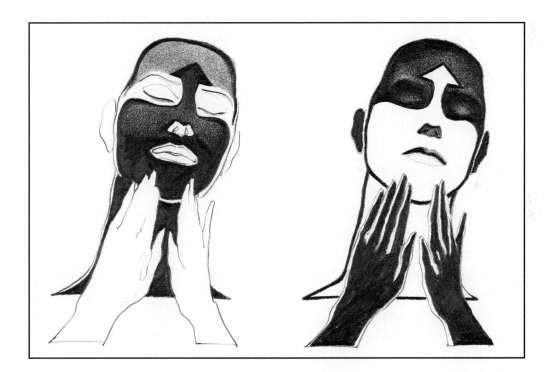

A final word on masks. Regardless of the mask you use, always apply a collagen and elastin-based cream after the mask. Collagen is a protein that is already in our skin—it exists in a jellylike form between the connective tissues. Elastin is one of the components in collagen. These are the things that keep our skin firm, toned and elastic. Collagen and elastin-based creams are expensive—but isn't it worth every penny for one literally to "save face"?

CONSTRUCTIVE LIE-DOWN

After you've had your bath and applied your mask the ideal thing to do is *nothing.* Lie down with your feet up while your mask dries. Place some cool, wrung-out teabags on the eyes. Camomile teabags are soothing. The tannic acid in regular teabags works, too. Either one will draw the puffiness from tired eyes.

Now just relax for ten-twenty minutes. That's all you really need to feel refreshed. And just think of all the wonderful things you're doing for yourself while you're resting. That's why I call this the Constructive Lie-down.

Believe it or not, ten minutes of rest can revive you more than a long, deep sleep, which might leave you feeling groggy. Napoleon fought his wars, existing on ten-minute catnaps. He never had time to sleep a whole night, so he'd take a few minutes here and there and would be totally revitalized and ready for battle. If a catnap worked for Napoleon, it will certainly work for you!

FABULOUS FRAGRANCE

I don't feel dressed, and I certainly don't feel dressed up, unless I have my fragrance on. Fragrance is such a personal, important element of style. I've been wearing the same fragrance forever—we're very close.

People always know when I've arrived because of my scent; "Ah, Marisa's here!" I consider it my calling card and as important as anything else I have on. If your friends smell your fragrance somewhere else, they are reminded of you. We all want to be remembered, don't we?

Perfume is so romantic. It's positively seductive. Men love it. Nothing is more provocative than creating a fragrant aura before being seen.

Besides jewels, fragrance is the most luxurious thing a woman can put on. And lots of it. Why bother unless you're really going to go all the way? I don't just put a little on my wrist and behind my ears, I spray it everywhere. After you've had your bath, mask and lie-down, isn't a big *whoosh* of fragrance the perfect touch?

There's no way that I can tell you what kind of fragrance to buy. Every

fragrance is unique and smells different on everyone. This is why picking a fragrance is so personal. However, most fragrances fall into one of the following categories:

Oriental: Sultry and exotic. Musk, civet, sandalwood and ambergris are used to produce this scent.

Spicy: Smells like it sounds, and the resulting fragrance is *haunting and nostalgic.* Cinnamon, cloves, ginger and spicy flowers are combined.

Citrus: Lively and refreshing. Lemons, oranges and limes are used to create this blend.

Floral Bouquets: Like smelling a nosegay of wonderful flowers. *Very romantic.* Flowers are blended with one another so that no one scent predominates.

Single Floral: One flower predominates this *dramatic* essence—usually gardenia, rose, jasmine, lily of the valley, or any fragrant flower.

Woodsy-Mossy: A *fresh, outdoorsy aroma* for earthy types. A distinct combination of herbs, ferns and oakmoss.

Forest Blend: Sophisticated. This blend is accented with oakmoss and amber, and floral, fruity or fresh green notes linger.

Instead of being overwhelmed at the fragrance counter, ask to try fragrances from a specific category. Are you the sultry type? Then try different orientals. Or maybe you see yourself as sophisticated. Test fragrances that are considered forest blends. Whatever you decide on, test it before you buy it. Ideally you can take a few samples home with you to find the fragrance that makes you feel the best.

Once you find your scent, develop a total fragrance wardrobe. For fragrance that lasts all night, layer your scent. Use your soap, body lotion, powder, perfume, cologne—the works! And do put your fragrance *everywhere.* Cotton balls soaked with your fragrance should be placed in your shoes, your lingerie drawers, suitcases, handbags—everywhere. You want everything you own to smell like you.

Tips:

❧ Instead of buying perfumed body lotion, I buy a very good body lotion with *Aloe vera* at the health food store, and add a few drops of my own perfume to it.

❧ Spray your perfume on the light bulbs—the heat will release its fragrance.

❧ Spray your hairbrush with your scent just before brushing. This is a marvelous way to freshen your hair if you don't have time to wash it.

❧ If your skin is dry you'll want to apply your fragrance immediately after the body lotion. The body lotion will act as a base and hold the scent.

Remember, your fragrance is your calling card—your personal signature. It's your silent friend that should be with you always. I always say no woman should be without her jewels, a sexy garter belt and her fragrance!

UNDERDRESSING

You've prepared your mind and you've prepared your body. Now the fun begins. It's time to get in the mood for dressing up. This means garter belts, beautiful bras and all of the lovely little lace nothings that make you feel great from head to toe.

I can't imagine putting on a fabulous dress over some sexless, ugly underwear. This is absurd. How can you capture the total feeling of dressing up unless you're wearing the most wonderful underdressings? Believe me, nothing will make you feel prettier than the joy of silk next to your skin.

When you have on some sexy lace tights and a pretty strapless bra you

move differently, you act differently—you act like a real woman. And when a man sees a garter and a little bit of stocking when a woman crosses her leg, it's a turn-on. After all, dressing up is about being feminine, pretty and a little bit seductive.

The proper underdressings determine the way your clothes fit and look. You always want a smooth, fluid look—as if your clothes are about to melt. When you walk there should be that little sigh of silk. And what could be prettier than a lace camisole top under a sheer silk blouse?

Dressing up is about undressing, too, whether it's for your husband, your lover, or just for yourself. Part of the magic of the evening is the beautiful panties, bras and stockings that you wear underneath. I want *him* to be as excited about me undressed as he was when I was dressed up.

6

FINISHING TOUCHES

IT'S YOUR NIGHT to shine, and a flawless face is the dramatic finish for a look that's dazzling! The simplest dress-up for your face is true red lipstick and black mascara. But no doubt you'll want to try an even more dramatic makeup statement.

Plan your evening makeup strategy in advance. You'll want your complexion to look flawless, your eyes smoldering and your lips sparkling. Evening makeup calls for more intense color, so you should collect nighttime makeup shades.

Proper makeup application and blending with the right tools help you

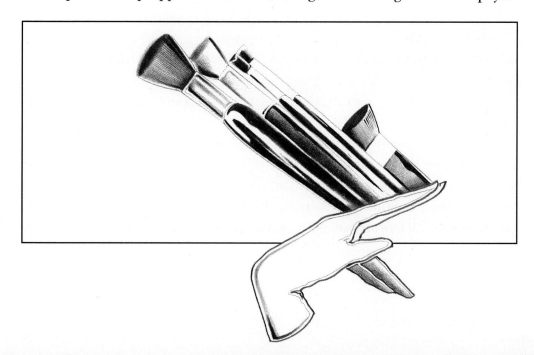

carry off a dramatic look that maintains natural qualities. Invest in a set of fluffy makeup brushes and tools. You'll need fluffy blusher brushes, a smaller eyeshadow brush, a thin lip brush, an eyebrow brush, an eyelash curler and a makeup sponge.

To create a clear "canvas" on which to apply makeup, cleanse the skin thoroughly and follow with a toner (for normal to dry skin) or an astringent (for normal to oily skin) to remove excess oils, refine and tighten large pores. Witch hazel will cut any puffiness. Follow with a light coating of moisturizer as a makeup base. Moisturizer helps colors go on smoothly, evenly; it softens the skin for superior blending and longer-lasting makeup.

For a super-gala, you might consider having your makeup done by a professional makeup artist. Many beauty salons and department stores offer makeup application at reasonable prices.

STARTING OFF—APPLYING FOUNDATION

To keep your complexion looking flawless, all night long, apply a sheer, lightweight foundation in a shade close to your natural skin tone. To achieve a sheer, natural-looking matte finish, dust your face lightly with a translucent powder. Extend foundation up to your hairline and down to your jawline, carefully blending color under the jaw. Don't extend the foundation down to your neck, because it may crease and smear as the evening goes on.

Oily skin will shine under evening lights, particularly if you'll be active—and perspiring. To prevent oils from breaking through your flawlessly made-up face, blot skin with an astringent before applying makeup, then apply the sheerest coating of nonoily foundation. Dust on loose, transparent powder to absorb excess foundation, then apply powder blush; apply more translucent powder to your finished face to set makeup and further remove oils.

If you have a *ruddy complexion,* tone it down by using a beige foundation that has yellow undertones. Avoid red and pink blusher and lip colors, and substitute shades such as peach, russet, mauve, coral.

If you have a *sallow complexion,* choose an ivory foundation with pink undertones. Avoid peach or coral makeup colors and any shades with a yellowish cast, and choose clear shades of red, pink or rose for lips and cheeks.

If your skin is dry or if you have fine lines that might become more noticeable as the evening wears on, use a heavy moisturizer before applying makeup. Let the moisturizer set into your skin for ten minutes; blot excess with facial tissue. Also choose a moisturizing foundation and cream blushers, then finish with translucent powder to blot up excess makeup oils that could crease into skin folds after a few hours' wear.

If your complexion is *pale or washed out,* give yourself a healthy glow. Apply blush to tops of cheekbones as usual, and lightly dust and blend color over temples, along the hairline at your forehead, along your jawline. If your complexion is very pale, add a healthy glow with an all-over face color (a liquid "color wash" or an "all-in-one" sheer colored powder, formulated for use all over the face and on eyes and lips). If you're using a fluid color wash, apply to skin in a thin, sheer layer before using foundation. If you're using a colored powder, apply lightly over foundation. Apply a deeper shade of blush to cheeks as usual, to emphasize the healthy glow.

CAMOUFLAGE TRICKS

Don't let late-night beauty flaws catch up with you. *If you tend to develop undereye circles* when you become tired, camouflage in advance: pat cream concealer—in a shade slightly lighter than your foundation—under eyes. Pat on only where circles usually appear. To blend, blot with fingertips in a tapping motion.

To ease undereye puffiness, take action just before applying makeup: lie down for ten minutes with cold, moist teabags or cotton pads soaked in ice water placed over closed eyes.

To ease fine lines and wrinkles that hinder your glamour look, use a concealing cream in a shade lighter than your skin tone. With a thin eyeliner brush, paint concealer along the creases of lines or wrinkles; blend with the brush, then apply foundation as usual, carefully blending it over concealer.

For a last-minute pimple, use foolproof camouflage. Wipe pimple with astringent or acne medication to dry oils; gently dab concealer over pimple and blend with fingertips until pimple is hidden. Brush on translucent powder to set concealer so the pimple doesn't break through later on in the evening.

For a last-minute hive: follow camouflage for pimples.

MAKING UP WITH COLOR

Opt for a soft, matte, natural finish to your face, as glitters and frost may look unnatural. But, when choosing colors, go for those with built-in shine. These colors aren't frosted—they have built-in shimmer that shows when the color catches the light, in eyeshadows, lipsticks, blushers.

Add extra dazzle to your evening face with a super-sheer, tinted translucent powder that makes your face glisten as it catches the light. These are available in pale pinks and soft gold shades. After you've applied all of your makeup, brush the powder over eyelids, tops of cheeks, temples; sweep powder over lips or mix with clear gloss and apply over your lip color.

CONSIDER THE LIGHTING

For an intimate, candlelit evening, choose delicate makeup colors that won't look overpowering under these conditions. Opt for a soft effect, but don't apply makeup too sparingly—you want to achieve a glowing warmth, but you don't want to look washed out under low lights. Choose natural, muted makeup colors, such as sienna, grape, smoky gray, olive, rust or bronze on eyes; russet, rose or peach on cheeks; pale pink or soft peach on lips.

For a brightly lit party, go for dazzle. Use dramatic, clear makeup colors that play up your best features, make you a standout. Good choices: amethyst, cobalt blue, teal, charcoal gray on eyes; fuchsia, rose or coral on cheeks; red, pink, ruby or soft orange on lips. The key to carrying off dramatic colors for a natural look is careful blending. If you're using creams, blend with your fingers. Use a makeup brush to blend powdered colors, feathering the edges so they "fade" into the skin. For further blending, brush translucent powder over each color after applying. Double-check makeup under various lightings to make sure there are no harsh lines. If it is daytime, check your makeup near a window—daylight will reveal any blending mistakes.

After applying foundation, use blusher to emphasize your cheekbones.

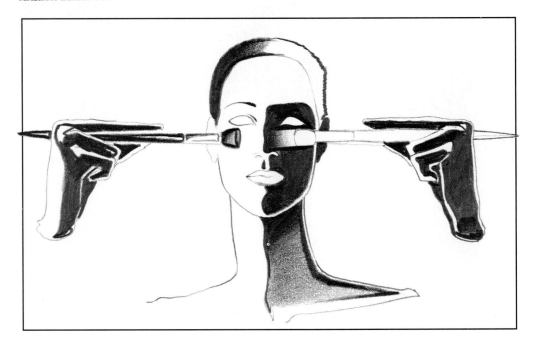

Apply your blusher along the cheekbones. (Stay away from contour powders; unless you're being photographed, they make you look too artificial.) Use *two* makeup brushes to apply blush on both cheeks simultaneously.

THE EYES HAVE IT

Make up your eyes for a dramatic effect. The eyes are like pearls, classic things that should be accented. Sexy nighttime eyes have big lids, deep sultry color in the crease, blended up and winged out to outer corners of eyes. To start, apply light, bright eyeshadow (such as pink, yellow, lavender) across lids to emphasize their size and shade. Using a deep, smoky eyeshadow (good choices are smoky blue, purple, copper) and an eyeshadow brush, apply color along crease of each eye, then apply more color to brush and sweep color up toward brow bone and out to outer corners for a winged effect that "lifts" the eyes. You might want to finish with a touch of blush on each eye to give a final blending (again, use two makeup brushes simultaneously).

Next, rim upper and lower lids with a smoky-black eye lining pencil. (If black is too harsh for your complexion, choose a smoky-blue or -gray pencil.) Line along upper and lower lids, following the shape of the lash line; smudge lines with a cotton swab for a soft, sultry effect. Extend the pencil lines

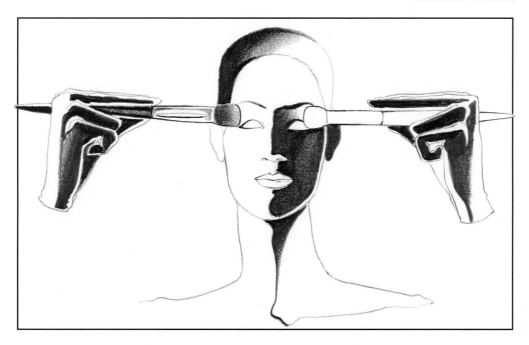

upward at outer corners of eyes for an alluring touch; smudge with cotton swab.

For long, "flirty" eyelashes, curl with an eyelash curler (clamp down on lashes, hold for five seconds and release). Apply a light coating of black lash-lengthening mascara, brush upper lashes up and lower lashes down with the mascara wand so that you coat all hairs; let dry; repeat twice. Black mascara will make your lashes stand out best and will bring your eyes right in focus.

For an eye-opening effect and to tame straggly brows, use an eyebrow brush to brush eyebrows straight up. To keep brows groomed in place, spray an eyebrow brush with hair spray; brush brows up into place.

If eyebrows are sparse, fill in spaces with an eyebrow pencil. Draw in "hairs" using short, feathery strokes, following the direction of natural hair growth.

The key to a well-dressed face for evening is strong, clear lip color that balances out the rest of the face. Choose a not-too-creamy lipstick, as it will last longer than creamy, glossy colors. Once you've chosen a lip color, apply it in this smudgeproof fashion so it lasts and lasts: Coat edges of lips with foundation; blend. Outline lips with a lip-lining pencil in a shade close to your lipstick color, following the natural shape of your lips; fill in with lipstick; blot with a tissue; repeat lipstick. Finish with a very sheer coating of clear lip gloss for shine.

For the most provocative evening mouth, play up your lips to the hilt by making them look larger than they are. Using a lip-lining pencil in a shade close to your lipstick, outline lips just outside your natural lip line; carefully fill in lips up to the lines by painting on lipstick with a lip brush.

Once you've applied your evening makeup, you must "set" it so that it lasts all evening long. Set your makeup with loose, translucent powder. This prevents makeup from streaking, fading, changing color, and it helps blend and smooth makeup colors. Using a clean fluffy powder brush, apply powder in upward sweeping motions, starting at the jawline and dusting up to forehead. Dust face with brush until powder is blended in; apply more powder if further blending is needed.

NAIL COLOR

Complete a well-dressed look with beautifully manicured nails. File nails into soft ovals or a slightly squared shape. Soak fingertips in warm, soapy water; dry fingers, then push back cuticles with an orangewood stick. Apply base coat, then nail color. For evening, bright red nail color is a top choice. If nails are short and red looks overpowering, choose pale pink, tan, rose or mauve. Don't leave nails without color; it's too casual for evening.

HAIR

I hate spending hours at the hairdresser's before a big night out. This can be avoided if you keep your hair cut in a style that works for you. It should be a style that you feel comfortable with and can manage yourself; something you can dress up at night.

If you're trying a new look for your hair, experiment in advance. For instance, if you're thinking of an "up do" and you rarely wear your hair up, try out the style by wearing it for a few hours, to see how it holds up and whether you will need to use more hairpins, or more or less hair spray.

Key your hairstyle to your clothes. For flowing, voluminous styles or oversized clothes, wear your hair full, loose and flowing, or in a full, dramatic

upsweep. For a tailored look, the options are open—wear hair full, smooth, or sleek and styled close to the head.

HAIR CONDITIONERS

Condition hair before styling, for body, manageability, shine.

If your hair is brittle, dull or damaged, give yourself a deep conditioning treatment during your grooming ritual (the type of conditioner you leave on for fifteen to thirty minutes) to add body, luster, to soften wiry or brittle hair, to tame frizzies and split ends.

If your hair is fine or limp, don't use a conditioner or creme rinse before styling, as these can make the hair softer so that it's difficult to style into place.

If you're planning to wear your hair in an elaborate style or pinned up off your face, don't shampoo or condition hair just before styling. Wash hair early in the day or the day before so natural oils, which help hold the hair in place, can accumulate.

BODY BUILDERS

If your hair is limp, if it lacks body or doesn't hold a style well, add "bulk" by backcombing with a brush. This is like teasing, but using a brush creates a soft, natural look. Lift up small sections of hair and tease underneath; fluff into place with fingers.

If you use a curling iron to add curl or body, make the results last longer. Curl a section of hair with the iron; remove curling-iron rod; clip the curl in place with a hairclip and repeat until all hair is curled. When hair cools remove clips; separate curls with fingers (brushing with a brush will remove some of the curl).

If you have frizzy hair, ease the frizz with a curling iron. Take a small section of hair, turn the curling iron at an angle and gently pull it through the hair. The heat from the curling iron closes hair cuticles to smooth frizzies.

If you're wearing your hair in a natural style but it lacks body, after shampooing, flip your head over and gently dry hair with a blow dryer, separating strands and tousling hair with fingertips. Flip head up and fluff hair into place with fingers, for a fringy, sexy, tousled look.

THE PERFECT FINISH

If you're wearing your hair in a special must-stay-in-place style, use a light misting of hair spray as the finishing touch. Hair spray is a necessity to hold an elaborate style in place. Choose a soft-hold hair spray that doesn't make the hair stiff.

If you're wearing your hair up and stray hairs stick out, spray a cotton ball with setting lotion or hair spray and rub it over the wisps until they're smoothed into place.

PLAYING UP YOUR HAIR'S TEXTURE

If your hair is straight or fine, style it simply since it won't hold an elaborate style or curly set well. If you plan to wear your hair up, such as in a chignon, roll or braid, set it first in pin curls or on hot rollers to texturize the hair for easier and longer-lasting styling.

If your hair is wavy or curly, it will look full of body if you wear it loose in its natural style. Wavy hair also has good holding power for more elaborate styling. If smooth, straight hair is more suited to your evening look, straighten hair by separating 1-inch sections of wet hair and gently pulling the hair with a brush as you apply heat from the blow dryer. Other options: pull a curling iron through thin sections of hair from roots to ends, or set hair on large hot rollers.

Any type of hair with heavy bangs is too casual for evening wear. If you have bangs, apply styling lotion or gel to fingertips, then flick bangs back so they blend in with the rest of your hair. Apply more styling lotion if more hold is needed. Pull a few wispy stray hairs onto forehead as a sexy finishing touch.

For curly or waved bobbed hair, if you want to wear your hair in a natural style, following the lines of the cut, accentuate the waves and curls. To do, briefly blow-dry wet hair as you fingerfluff it away from the face toward the back of your head. When hair is just damp, clip waves or curls into place using hairclips; spray on setting lotion. When hair is dry, remove clips. Don't brush hair, as you'll disturb the wave pattern.

HIGH STYLING—SHORT HAIR

For straight, chin-length hair: Work with your hairstyle—dry hair as usual, then add bounce, swing and softness by curving the ends of hair under, using medium-sized hot rollers. To do, separate hair into 1-inch sections and roll just the ends of the hair up on roller. Hold roller in place with hand for twenty seconds; remove. Repeat until ends of hair are softly curved under all around. Brush any bangs off of face and arrange wisps onto forehead.

Another option: for an extremely high-fashion look, wear hair stick-straight all around. To do, blow-dry hair while pulling sections out straight with a brush. Brush bangs off of face and pull spiky wisps onto forehead.

Short-short hair: Give your hair extra volume and direction for added glamour. To do, towel-dry hair, then blow-dry as you use fingers to fluff hairs away from face toward back of head. Apply styling lotion to fingertips, run fingers through hair to style into place; let hair dry. If your hair is straight and needs more coaxing, towel-dry hair, then roll small sections up on a round brush, going away from the face, and blow-dry until dry; release brush, fingerfluff hair into place.

If you want your hair to look curly all around, set entire head on small hot rollers, or, if hair is too short for rollers, cut 1-inch strips of fabric, such as cotton, and wind hair around the fabric; clip into place with hairpins. When setting, divide hair into small sections; pull each section forward, then roll back onto roller. Remove rollers, but don't brush hair. Separate strands with fingers and fluff into place. Mist hair lightly with water to expand curl; spray with hair spray to help hold the set.

For a longer-hair look, apply styling lotion or gel to slightly damp hair. Comb hair back and straight away from face; pin with hairpins about 2 inches away from hairline all around to keep hair smooth, then set top crown section of hair on small rollers or curl with a curling iron; fingerfluff into place.

Another longer-hair look: Flip head over, apply styling lotion or gel to hair with fingers, smoothing hair up from nape of neck toward crown. Secure hair smoothly under crown with hairpins. Flip head up. Set hair from crown to hairline at forehead into pin curls and leave for thirty minutes, or use small hot rollers for ten minutes. Remove curlers. Tousle hair with fingers to separate curls—do not brush; mist with hair spray or styling lotion to hold the set.

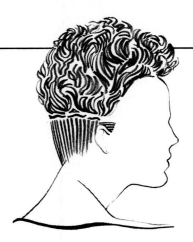

For a full, curly look, pull hair smoothly back off of the face with a flexible comb (a comblike implement that fits around the head like a headband to grip hair back, available at variety stores) or a headband. Pull out tiny wisps around hairline to frame face. Curl hair with a curling iron for a sexy softness.

For super sophistication, wear short hair slicked back, with tiny wisps falling softly onto your forehead. To do, coat damp hair with setting gel or styling lotion; comb hair straight back; let dry.

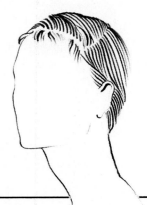

HIGH STYLING—LONG HAIR

For a very provocative look, brush wet hair over to one side of head; pin with hairpins to secure; then dry hair with a blow dryer. Next, rub styling lotion between hands, and run hands through hair to "set" into place; mist with styling lotion or hair spray.

If hair is long and full of body, wear it loose and flowing for a fuss-free, evening look. For added glamour, pull hair back off of one side of your face and secure with a jeweled hair comb.

Create a softly rolled style while maintaining a long-hair look. To do, part hair from ear to ear; grasp the front section and brush it over to the right side of your face. Twist the section of hair and wind into a soft roll; pin in place. Place an elaborate chignon stick into the roll. Brush remaining hair so it falls softly over your shoulders.

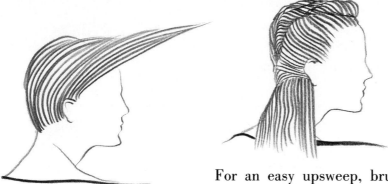

For an easy upsweep, brush damp hair forward to forehead; grasp hair at scalp and twist from end to end. Fold twist back along head; pin into place. Variation: leave loose hair at nape. Let hair dry, then mist with hair spray.

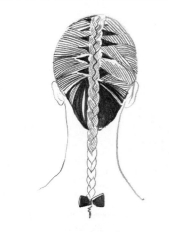

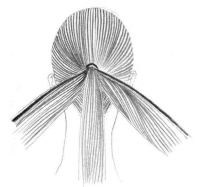

A French braid is a most alluring and fashionable look for long hair, and an ideal way to style fine hair that lacks body. You can French braid your hair starting at the forehead, going down along the center of your head, or starting at the crown and braiding down to the nape. Or you can braid hair on each side of your head separately and join braids at the nape. To do, take one section of hair and divide into three parts. Braid the three parts as usual, and after the first intertwining, add more hair from underneath into each of the three parts of hair and work it into the braid as you intertwine the pieces again. Repeat sequence to neckline; braid remaining hair. Secure braid with an elastic band and secure hair along braid with hairpins.

For really long hair, make a regular braid dressed up with ribbon! Cut two long strands of ribbon, silk cord or chain, in a color keyed to clothes. Make a ponytail where the braid will start (at top or sides of head or nape of neck) and secure with a disposable rubber band. Separate sections of hair to be braided into three parts; pin ribbon close to scalp on the outside of the two outer sections of hair so that ribbon will show as you braid. Start braiding hair as usual, crossing over the two sections of hair with the ribbon and the one without ribbon. Knot ends of braids using ribbon, trim off excess. Cut the rubber band you used to make the ponytail so braid hangs softly.

A great way to accent long hair is with jewelry!
A few options:

Pull all hair up to crown or off to one side of head and secure in a ponytail, with an elastic band. Slip a bangle bracelet (or bracelets) through length of hair. To secure in place, use a needle and thread that matches your hair color to sew bangle onto elastic band or through your hair.

Instead of using a bangle, make a ponytail and wind a strand of pearls, beads or gold chain around base of ponytail.

Gather hair into a ponytail; secure with an elastic band, then take a long length of metallic cord or ribbon and wrap around the ponytail as many times as you like. Make a knot at end of cord; trim excess.

For any length hair, create a truly dramatic effect by wearing a head wrap. Use an oblong scarf or cut a length of suede, leather, linen, metallic or mesh fabric. Wrap fabric around your hair—close to your hairline—turban-style—and knot fabric at the nape of your neck. Let remaining hair flow over sides of "turban," or you can keep your hair pinned up; pull wisps onto forehead.

Or really go all out and wrap your head in a turban as shown on page 134. When I lived in India I kept my head wrapped in one all the time. I lived by the sea, and my hair was always frizzy. The look for the time was *straight*, so my solution was the turban. I think it's a terrific look!

Consider accenting any hairstyle with fresh flowers. For short hair, pin a flower behind the ear, or pull hair back on one side and secure with a hair comb to which you've attached a flower. For long hair, pull hair back on one side of face and pin in place; slip a flower stem through the pins. If you're wearing your hair up, such as in a roll or knot, secure a flower into the side of the style with hairpins.

Feathers are another flashy way to ornament hair, but they should be small so the look remains elegant but understated. Pin feather to a hair comb and tuck into hair at one side of your face, or secure feather into a ponytail or at the top of an upsweep.

A FINAL WORD—DRESSED UP

DRESSING UP is making the effort and creating whatever illusion you fancy. It's a time to express your moods and whims—it's your chance to make a personal statement. Think of it as a silent way to proclaim, "Here I am!" And dressing up should be fun—otherwise, what's the point?

Remember all the fun we had dressing up when we were children? We'd break into Mommy's closets and vanity table and go at it with wild abandon. This is how dressing up should be for you now—throw yourself into it with the same childlike, imaginative joy! Yes, joy. There should be joy involved with every aspect of it, not anxiety and terror.

And just how does a woman get the courage to really dress up? By appreciating herself and believing in herself. Don't be afraid to show the great you that deserves to be displayed. After all, dressing up is a woman's greatest moment.

Once you begin dressing up, enjoy every part of it. (What other time in your busy life do you ever really get to indulge in being a woman?) Enjoy shopping and exploring all the possibilities that your clothes hold. Appreciate the thrill of a special hairstyle created *just for tonight* or the fun of discovering some shimmery new eye makeup. And isn't it wonderful that those old jewels

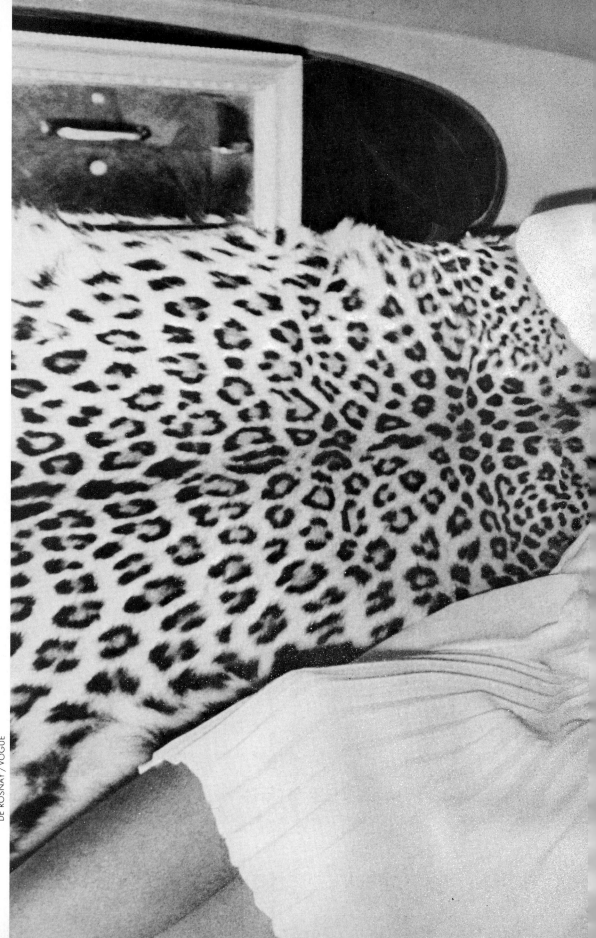

*Here I am with my husband, Richard, dressed for the Valentino party at the
Metropolitan Museum of Art.*

you've never been able to wear suddenly have a place and, in fact, are creating a fantastic look you never thought possible.

Yes, drab and dreary are safe—but how boring! If you take my philosophy for dressing up, you won't just look good; you'll be stunning. The great clothes and jewels you wear will give you a strong sense of yourself and a whole new attitude. Every woman should feel marvelous inside and out, and that's just what dressing up is about.

I say, go for it when you're dressing up. Pull out all the stops and don't balk or hesitate. Do it with gusto. Do it with flair. And have fun! With a little bit of *doing,* the evening is yours for the asking.